Student Feedback

Student Feedback

The cornerstone to an effective quality assurance system in higher education

EDITED BY
CHENICHERI SID NAIR AND
PATRICIE MERTOVA

CP

CHANDOS
PUBLISHING

Oxford Cambridge New Delhi

Chandos Publishing
TBAC Business Centre
Avenue 4
Station Lane
Witney
Oxford OX28 4BN
UK
Tel: +44 (0) 1993 848726
Email: info@chandospublishing.com
www.chandospublishing.com

Chandos Publishing is an imprint of Woodhead Publishing Limited

Woodhead Publishing Limited
80 High Street,
Sawston,
Cambridge CB22 3HJ
UK
www.woodheadpublishing.com

First published in 2011

ISBN:
978 1 84334 573 2

Typeset by RefineCatch Limited, Bungay, Suffolk
Printed in the UK and USA.

Printed in the UK by 4edge Limited - www.4edge.co.uk

Contents

List of figures and tables

Figures

Tables

About the authors

Phillip Adams is Evaluations Manager at the Centre for Higher Education Quality (CHEQ), Monash University, Australia. Mr Adams's expertise in the field of evaluations is in infrastructure solutions for the efficient functioning of feedback systems. He has significant knowledge and expertise in developing technological solutions to a range of equity and accessibility issues. He has published a number of related articles and presented at relevant conferences. Apart from his work in evaluations, he has extensive experience in project management, computer system design and programming, and secondary teaching.

Lorraine Bennett is an Associate Professor at the University of Ballarat. Dr Bennett provides leadership for academic development at the University of Ballarat in regional Australia and is the Project Leader for an Australian Learning and Teaching Council Leadership Project at Monash University, Australia. Dr Bennett has extensive experience in leadership, having held a large number of senior roles in higher education and local and state government. The main focus of her work is on the scholarship of learning and teaching and spans staff development, teaching and research. Her special areas of interest include leadership capacity building, organisational reform, change management, strategic planning, policy development, quality improvement and internationalisation.

Denise Chalmers is Winthrop Professor and Director of the Centre for the Advancement of Teaching and Learning (CATL) at the University of Western Australia (UWA). She has worked in higher education for 25 years and is currently leading a national Australian Learning and Teaching Council (ALTC) project on rewarding and recognising quality teaching and learning through developing teaching and learning indicators in Australian universities. She is President of the Council of Australian Directors for Academic Development (CADAD). Prior to this, Denise was a foundation Director at the Carrick Institute for Learning and Teaching in Higher Education (renamed the Australian Learning and Teaching Council), a national organisation established to promote the quality of teaching and learning in Australian higher education, with specific responsibility for Awards, Fellowships and International Links. In her previous position as Director of the Teaching and Educational Development Institute (TEDI) at the University of Queensland, Australia, she was responsible for supporting the enhancement of teaching and learning, professional development, e-learning resource development and evaluation of teaching across the University.

Hamish Coates leads higher education research at the Australian Council for Educational Research (ACER). Over the last decade, he has designed and led numerous projects that have influenced international, national and institutional research, policy and practice. Dr Coates' research and publications focus on the definition, measurement and evaluation of educational processes, contexts and outcomes. His active interests include large-scale educational evaluation, tertiary education policy, learner engagement, institutional leadership, quality assurance and assessment methodology. He teaches research methods at all levels, works routinely with national and institutional advisory groups, publishes and presents widely. He has worked with all Australian universities and numerous training organisations, serves on a number of editorial boards, has been a consultant to the World Bank and OECD, and has held visiting fellowships at the University of Michigan and UNESCO's International Institute for Educational Planning.

Hadina Habil is Associate Professor in the Department of Modern Languages, Faculty of Management and Human Resource Development, Universiti Teknologi Malaysia, Skudai, Johor. Her research interests are in the areas of English for Specific Purposes, Business Communication, Computer Mediated Communication and Language and Communication. She has presented papers in conferences nationally and internationally and has published a number of articles in related areas.

Lee Harvey is Professor at Copenhagen Business School in Denmark. Prior to that, he was Director of Research at the Higher Education Academy in the UK. He also established and was Director of both the Centre for Research into Quality at the University of Central England in Birmingham and the Centre for Research and Evaluation at Sheffield Hallam University, UK. Lee has wide experience in social science research as a research methodologist and social philosopher. His areas of expertise include higher education policy, with particular focus on issues of quality, employability and student feedback. He has published widely, with over

35 books and research monographs and over 120 articles in international journals, books and compendiums. He has been a quality adviser to institutions across the world. He is regularly invited to be a keynote speaker at major international conferences.

Katarina Mårtensson is an academic developer at Lund University Centre for Educational Development, Sweden. She runs teacher training courses for academic staff and supports academic staff at all levels in the faculties with an effort to promote and initiate academic development. Currently, she is also responsible for initiatives involving leadership in academia. Together with Torgny Roxå, she has been responsible for a national project in Sweden to support professional development for academic developers. Her main research interests and publications include strategic educational development and social perspectives on learning and cultural change in higher education institutions.

Patricie Mertova is currently a Research Fellow in the Department of Education, University of Oxford, England. Dr Mertova was previously a Research Officer at the University of Queensland, and, prior to that, a Research Fellow in the Centre for the Advancement of Learning and Teaching (CALT) and the Centre for Higher Education Quality (CHEQ), Monash University, Australia. She has recently completed her PhD, focusing on the academic voice in higher education quality. She has research expertise in the areas of higher education and higher education quality. Her background is also in the areas of linguistics, translation, cross-cultural communication and foreign languages.

Chenicheri Sid Nair is Professor of Higher Education Development with the Centre for Advancement of Teaching and Learning at the University of Western Australia (UWA). Prior to his appointment to UWA, he was Quality Adviser (Research and Evaluation) at the Centre for Higher Education Quality (CHEQ) at Monash University, Australia. He has extensive expertise in the area of quality development and evaluation, and he also has considerable editorial experience. Currently, he is Associate Editor of the *International Journal of Quality Assurance in Engineering and Technology Education* (IJQAETE). Prior to this, he was a Managing Editor of the *Electronic Journal of Science Education* (EJSE). Professor Nair is also an international consultant in a number of countries in the areas of quality and stakeholder feedback.

Fernando F. Padró is Associate Professor in the EdD Programme in Educational Leadership at Cambridge College, Cambridge, Massachusetts, USA. He has been actively involved in researching the impact of the field of quality on school and university organisational behaviour and policy for more than 25 years. He has written a number of articles pertinent to issues of quality, quality assurance and accreditation in higher education. He has also presented on these subjects at over 50 conferences and similar forums in Australia, Europe and the USA. He has been a Malcolm Baldrige National Quality Award Examiner in the USA as well as a Peer Reviewer with the Academic Quality Improvement Programme (AQIP) project and is currently responsible for his College's School of Education Teacher Education Accreditation Council (TEAC) accreditation process. Presently, he is the Chair of the American Society for Quality's (ASQ) Higher Education Advisory Committee and ASQ's Education Division Vice-Chair for International Activities.

Marlia Puteh is currently a senior lecturer at the College of Science and Technology, Universiti Teknologi Malaysia International Campus, Kuala Lumpur, Malaysia. She has a PhD from Monash University, Australia and also an MA in English Language Studies from Universiti Kebangsaan Malaysia. Her areas of interest are quality assurance in higher education, higher education policies, English language studies and online learning.

Torgny Roxå has been an academic developer since 1989. Currently, he is an academic developer in the Faculty of Engineering at Lund University, Sweden. His main interest is in Strategic Educational Development in Higher Education, a cultural approach where the essentialist and the socio-cultural perspectives are used in combination. He has developed several major measures for change, both at Lund University and nationally in Sweden. He holds a Master's degree in Higher Education from Griffith University, Australia.

James Williams is Senior Researcher at the Centre for Research into Quality, Birmingham City University, UK. Dr Williams's research focuses on the broad experience of students in higher education, at national and international levels, and he has published widely in the field. Much of this is drawn from his experience in collecting and using institutional student feedback. He regularly presents papers and conducts workshops at international conferences on this subject and has coordinated a number of institutional student satisfaction surveys since 2004. All this is part of his interest in how to use the students' own experiences to improve quality in higher education. He is Associate Editor of the international journal, Quality in Higher Education. As a historian by training, he continues to publish within his original field of Tudor cultural history and is currently researching the history of HE in the non-university sector.

Preface

Student feedback has been a contested area of higher education quality for over a decade. Initially, it was utilised primarily as a teaching performance management tool, which many lecturers have perceived as highly controversial. Gradually, feedback instruments started being recognised as tools which may enhance teaching and learning, rather than just a monitoring tool for underperforming or otherwise unpopular lecturers.

This book aims to highlight the developments and emerging trends in the student feedback domain. The book consists of nine chapters, highlighting not only the expansion in the use of student feedback in higher education, but also specific issues relating to university leadership in this area, facets of feedback administration and the use of the results in institutions worldwide. There is a common theme running through a majority of the chapters and that is the recognition of the need to act on student feedback and thus improve teaching and learning in universities.

In this publication, we draw upon international perspectives on the importance and use of student feedback in the higher education setting. The book not only looks at the current literature on student feedback but it also focuses on experiences of the individual authors, some of whom have covered international perspectives and trends as well as their individual national circumstances. In addition to being experts in their particular disciplines, many of the contributors are also researchers and practitioners in the area of student feedback.

In brief, the parts and chapters are:

Part 1: Overview

Chapter 1: The nexus of feedback and improvement

Lee Harvey of the Copenhagen Business School (Denmark) discusses the landscape of factors impacting on student feedback in higher education. The chapter situates student feedback in the current higher education context internationally and provides an overview of the debates surrounding the topic. In particular, it underlines the fact that student surveys and feedback have little effect without being incorporated in a strategy involving acting on student feedback and also informing students of the actions taken to motivate them to participate in feedback provision in the future.

Part 2: International perspectives

Chapter 2: Student feedback in the US and global contexts

Fernando Padró of Cambridge College, USA, provides a glimpse of the controversies, dilemmas and issues of using student feedback from the perspective of performance management of units and staff in the USA. The chapter points to the abundance of surveys currently utilised for various aspects of higher education, while underlining the significance of incorporating student feedback into systematic institutional decision-making. The chapter further argues that the challenges may be found in the purposes for which student feedback surveys are utilised. Fernando highlights the potential for the clash of cultures between external stakeholders (who tend to perceive tertiary education as a service) and academics (who tend to view tertiary education as a transformative and developmental process).

Chapter 3: Student feedback in higher education: a Malaysian perspective

Marlia Puteh and Hadina Habil from the Universiti Teknologi Malaysia situate student feedback in the Malaysian higher education context, in which the government has institutionalised collecting student feedback with the aim of enhancing tertiary teaching and learning. The chapter indicates that the practice of collecting student feedback is relatively new in the Malaysian higher education context, and has faced a significant amount of resistance from academics, and institutions have also faced a number of technical issues related to establishing effective evaluation systems. The chapter documents these issues within the context of one higher education institution.

Chapter 4: Improving university teaching through student feedback: a critical investigation

Torgny Roxå and Katarina Mårtensson of Lund University, Sweden, describe the way in which student evaluations are handled in the Swedish higher education context. The chapter provides a case study of one university in Sweden, which illustrates the need for an effective evaluation system that encompasses good data collection and the use of the data resulting from the feedback. The chapter supports the argument made in a number of other chapters in this book that student feedback surveys may be perceived as burdensome to administer and also to provide, unless they are acted upon collaboratively and communicated among university leadership, programme leaders, lecturers and students.

Chapter 5: The practice and use of student feedback in the Australian national and university context

Denise Chalmers from the University of Western Australia provides an Australian perspective on the use of student feedback in quality assurance at the local and national levels. This chapter also touches upon the changes taking place at universities with respect to the use of such feedback as a quality performance measure. In addition, she highlights the integration of such data from 'internal university feedback surveys with the national surveys to provide a more detailed and multilayered profile of their students' experiences'.

Part 3: Tools and administration

Chapter 6: Tools for effective student feedback

Hamish Coates from the Australian Council for Educational Research (ACER) reviews a range of instruments utilised for collecting student feedback for quality assurance and enhancement purposes. His chapter investigates the relationship between internal and external quality management and uncovers a number of discontinuities. The chapter concludes with some prospects for taking more concerted approaches to quality management in tertiary institutions.

Chapter 7: Web-based or paper-based surveys: a quandary?

Lorraine Bennett from Monash University and Chenicheri Sid Nair from the University of Western Australia investigate the types of platforms universities use for administering surveys. In particular, the authors examine the benefits and drawbacks in utilising paper-based versus online surveys in relation to student response rates. The discussion in this chapter is based on the experiences in a large research-intensive university.

Chapter 8: Inclusive practice in student feedback systems

Chenicheri Sid Nair from the University of Western Australia, Phillip Adams from Monash University and Patricie Mertova from the University of Oxford initiate a discussion concerning inclusive practice in student feedback systems. In particular, the chapter discusses the need to recognise the disadvantage of some students and to have systems that include all participants in an institution. The authors further reinforce the significance of communication with students when seeking feedback from them: before, during and after the surveying process.

Chapter 9: Action and the feedback cycle

James Williams from Birmingham City University, United Kingdom, explores the action cycle in the feedback process. In particular, this chapter draws upon cases at a number of universities that use the Student Satisfaction Approach in their feedback mechanism. The chapter reiterates a pivotal point: that there is a need not only to take action on what is revealed from the feedback but to communicate effectively back to the students the actions that have resulted. The author highlights the current tensions between the intentions of many UK institutions of listening to the student voice and acting on it and the government's pressures for competition based on league tables.

In summary, this book suggests that student surveys utilised for quality enhancement and quality assurance purposes are here to stay. The prevailing themes running through many of these chapters are the ever-present tensions and disconnects between the use of student feedback for assurance versus enhancement purposes in a majority of higher education systems covered in this book. Other recurring themes of the book include the need for action on student feedback, communication of actions to students as well as a need for an ongoing debate with students. Although these arguments were given from a range of national platforms, they were directed towards the more international and global nature of utilising student feedback in higher education.

Chenicheri Sid Nair and Patricie Mertova

Part 1
Overview

The nexus of feedback and improvement

Lee Harvey

Abstract: Student feedback on their experience is ubiquitous but is only useful if valued and acted upon. Generic student surveys are often used but more fine-grained surveys are more effective in informing improvement initiatives. To make an effective contribution to internal improvement processes, students' views need to be integrated into a regular and continuous cycle of analysis, action and report back to students on action taken. Student feedback often assumes a consumerist view rather than a transformative view of learning and hence a focus on facilities and teaching rather than learning. As well as feedback *from* students on their learning environment, feedback *to* students on their work and progress is vital for transformative learning. Feedback to students is often poor and there are various ways to improve such feedback and hence empower students as effective autonomous learners.

Key words: valuing student views; feedback cycle; transformative learning; improvement; feedback to students.

Introduction

Student feedback on aspects of their experience is ubiquitous. Indeed, it is now expected. The recent Parliamentary Select Committee report in the UK (House of Commons, 2009) concluded, *inter alia*, with the following student comment: 'What contributes to a successful university experience is an institution which actively seeks, values and acts on student feedback' (p. 131).

Carr et al. (2005) commented:

> Student surveys are perhaps one of the most widely used methods of evaluating learning outcomes (Leckey and Neill, 2001: 24) and teaching quality. Students may have a certain bias which influences their responses, however, the student perspective is advantageous for being much more immediate than analyses of, for example, completion and retention rates. Further, the view presented in the survey is that of the learner, 'the person participating in the learning process' (Harvey, 2001). Harvey also identified the value in the richness of information that can be obtained through the use of student surveys (Harvey, 2001).

Much earlier, Astin (1982), for example, had argued that students are in a particularly good position to comment upon programmes of study and thus to assist institutions to improve their contribution to student development. Hill (1995) later argued, from a student perspective, that students are 'often more acutely aware of problems, and aware more quickly' than staff or visiting teams of peers; which is, 'perhaps, the primary reason for student feedback on their higher education to be gathered and used regularly' (p. 73).

However, this has not always been the case. Twenty years ago, systematic feedback from students about their experience in higher education was a rarity. With the expansion of the university sector, the concerns with quality and the growing 'consumerism' of higher education, there has been a significant growth of, and sophistication in, processes designed to collect views from students.

Most higher education institutions, around the world, collect some type of feedback from students about their experience of higher education. 'Feedback' in this sense refers to the expressed opinions of students about the service they receive as students. This may include: perceptions about the learning and teaching; the learning support facilities, such as libraries and computing facilities; the learning environment, such as lecture rooms, laboratories, social space and university buildings; support facilities including refectories, student accommodation, sport and health facilities and student services; and external aspects of being a student, such as finance, car parking and the transport infrastructure.

Student views are usually collected in the form of 'satisfaction' feedback in one way or another; albeit some surveys pretend that by asking 'agree–disagree' questions they are not actually asking about satisfaction with provision. Sometimes, but all too rarely, there are specific attempts to obtain student views on how to improve specific aspects of provision or on their views about potential or intended future developments.

The reaction to student views also seems to have shifted. Baxter (1991) found that over half the respondents in a project he reported experienced improved job satisfaction and morale and almost all were influenced by student evaluation to change their teaching practice. Massy and French (2001) also stated, in their review of the teaching quality in Hong Kong, that 'staff value and act upon student feedback' and are 'proactive in efforts to consult with students' (p. 38). However, more recently, Douglas and Douglas (2006) suggested that staff have very little faith in student feedback questionnaires, whether module or institutional. This is not so surprising when student feedback processes tend to be bureaucratised and disconnected from the everyday practice of students and teaching staff; a problem that is further compounded by a lack of real credit and reward for good teaching.

Ironically, although feedback from students is assiduously collected in many institutions, it is less clear that it is used to its full potential. Indeed, a question mark hangs over the value and usefulness of feedback from students as collected in most institutions. The more data institutions seek to collect, the more cynical students seem to become and the less valid the information generated and the less the student view is taken seriously. Church (2008) remarked that 'students can often feel ambivalent about completing yet another course or module questionnaire. This issue becomes particularly acute when students are not convinced of the value of such activity – particularly if they don't know what resulted from it.'

In principle, feedback from students has two main functions: internal information to guide improvement; and external information for potential students and other stakeholders. In addition, student feedback data can be used for control and accountability purposes when it is part of external quality assurance processes. This is not discussed here as it is in fact a trivial use of important data, which has as its first priority improvement of the learning experience.

Improvement

It is not always clear how views collected from students fit into institutional quality improvement policies and processes. To be effective in quality improvement, data collected from surveys and peer reviews must be transformed into information that can be used within an institution to effect change.

To make an effective contribution to internal improvement processes, views of students need to be integrated into a regular and continuous cycle of analysis, reporting, action and feedback, be it at the level of an individual taught unit or at the institutional level (Figure 1.1). In many cases it is not always clear that there is a means to close the loop between data collection and effective action, let alone feedback to students on action taken, even within the context of module feedback questionnaires. Closing the loop is, as various commentators have suggested, an important, albeit neglected, element in the student feedback process (Ballantyne, 1997; Powney and Hall, 1998; Watson, 2003; Palermo, 2004; Walker-Garvin, undated). Watson (2003) argued that closing the loop and providing information on action taken encourages participation in further research and increases confidence in results, as well as it being ethical to debrief respondents. It also encourages the university management to explain how they will deal with the highlighted issues.

| **Figure 1.1** | Satisfaction cycle |

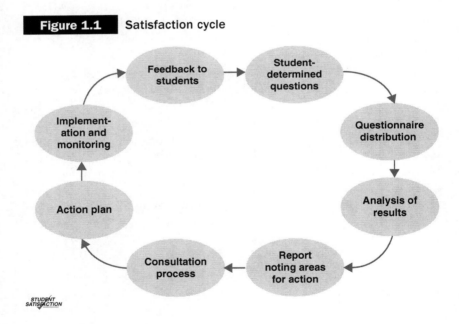

Making effective use of feedback requires that the institution has in place an appropriate system at each level that:

- identifies and delegates responsibility for action;
- encourages ownership of plans of action;

- requires accountability for action taken or not taken;
- communicates back to students on what has happened as a result of their feedback (closes the loop);
- commits appropriate resources.

As Yorke (1995) noted, 'The University of Central England has for some years been to the fore in systematising the collection and analysis of data in such a way as to suggest where action might be most profitably directed (Mazelan et al., 1992)' (p. 20). However, establishing an effective system is not an easy task, which is why so much data on student views is not used to effect change, irrespective of the good intentions of those who initiate the enquiries. There is much latent inertia in seeing through the implications of collecting student feedback, which is reflected in student indifference to many feedback processes. It is more important to ensure an appropriate action cycle than it is to have in place mechanisms for collecting data. Williams (2002) extends this and maintains that it is more important to focus attention on the use of results and sustaining change rather than on the results themselves.

External information

In an era when there is an enormous choice available to potential students, the views of current students offer a useful information resource. Yet very few institutions make the outcomes of student feedback available externally. The University of Central England in Birmingham (UCE) (now Birmingham City University), which, as Rowley (1996: 246) said, 'pioneered' student feedback, was also exceptional in publishing, from its inception in 1988, the results of its institution-wide student feedback survey, which reported to the level of faculty and major programmes.[1] Institutions abroad that have implemented the UCE Student Satisfaction approach, including Auckland University of Technology (Horsburgh, 1998) and Lund University (Torper, 1997) have published the results. However, the norm in Britain is to consider that student views are confidential to the university.

Preoccupation with surveys

There is a debilitating assumption that feedback from students should be sought via a survey, usually a questionnaire. More than a decade ago,

Rowley (1996) noted that: 'Commitment to the continuing improvement of quality within institutions has led to the collection of feedback from students. Questionnaires are the prime tool used in the process' (p. 224).

The following sections explore typical questionnaire approaches but prior to that, an important note on alternative approaches. Questionnaires, indeed surveys of any sort, are very poor ways of collecting student feedback. First, they are indirect and often there is no clear indication to students of the value or use of the data provided. Secondly, and more importantly, surveys rarely, if ever, provide a nuanced understanding of student concerns, issues and acknowledgements. Thirdly, because of this lack of nuanced understanding, surveys usually end up with open comments that seem to be in direct opposition to the generally satisfactory ratings from closed questions. This is because the structure is such that students tend, in the main, to use the open comments to raise complaints or concerns that the closed questions do not adequately address. Fourthly, most surveys do not explore how improvements could be made as the student view on appropriate improvements is rarely directly asked and, usually, the students have not been involved in the design of the survey in the first place. Hence, there is a significant degree of student indifference as the surveys seem to be simply providing a legitimation for inaction.

A much more useful means of exploring the student perspective is through direct dialogue. This can occur in many ways, for example, though face-to-face discussion groups within the classroom, 'chaired' by the lecturer, a student or an external facilitator (with or without the lecturer present). These may be ad hoc discussions, formally-minuted scheduled events, or based on focus group sessions. Discussions may be conducted virtually, through blogs, online discussion groups or webinars, for example.

The representative system in which students are members of committees at all levels also provides a means for obtaining feedback, as also does the formal complaints system. Rowley (1996) noted that:

> In addition to the formal questionnaire-based survey many institutions make use of complaints systems and suggestion boxes, which provide useful feedback, but it is difficult for managers to gauge the extent to which these are indicative of user opinion, or are representative of only the vociferous minority. However, these can be used alongside annual satisfaction surveys, not least because they provide a quicker means of communication than a survey on an annual cycle. (p. 248)

However, most valuable, at least for the teaching team, is the informal feedback provided impromptu in classes, during tutorials, via corridor or coffee-break chats or through e-mails. This informal feedback is 'student-centred', to the point, and timely. It may be from Rowley's 'vociferous minority', but a reflective lecturer can discern when there is a genuine issue for consideration and when someone is, for example, venting frustration.

However, this requires that staff (academics, administrators and managers) listen to what they are being told rather than ignoring it; reconstituting it as unrealistic, rebutting criticisms, or assuming students do not know what is best for them, or any of the other numerous techniques adopted to ensure that they do not hear the unwelcome messages.

Types of surveys

The predominant 'satisfaction' survey takes five forms:

- institution-level satisfaction with the total student experience or a specified sub-set;
- faculty-level satisfaction with provision;
- programme-level satisfaction with the learning and teaching and related aspects of a particular programme of study (for example, BA Business Studies);[2]
- module-level feedback on the operation of a specific module or unit of study (for example, Introduction to Statistics);
- teacher-appraisal by students.

Institution-level satisfaction

Systematic, institution-wide student feedback about the quality of the total educational experience was an area of growing activity in many countries. However, innovations in this area have been thwarted by the introduction of banal national surveys designed to provide simplistic comparative data by which institutions can be compared. The upshot is more concern with ranking tables than with addressing underlying issues (Williams and Cappuccini-Ansfield, 2007). The mock accountability and misleading public information of such national surveys constitutes a fatuous waste of money and effort.

Institution-level satisfaction surveys are almost always based on questionnaires, which mainly consist of questions with pre-coded answers augmented by one or two open questions. In the main, these institution-wide surveys are (or should be) undertaken by a dedicated unit with expertise in undertaking surveys, producing easily interpretable results to schedule.

Institution-wide surveys tend to encompass most of the services provided by the university and are not to be confused with standardised institutional forms seeking feedback at the programme or module level (discussed below). In the main, institution-wide surveys seek to collect data that provides information for management designed to encourage action for improvement and, at their best, the surveys are based on the student perspective rather than on the preconceived notions of managers. Such surveys can also provide an overview of student opinion for internal and external accountability purposes, such as reporting to boards of governors or as evidence to quality auditors.

The way the results are used varies. In some cases there is a clear reporting and action mechanism. In others, it is unclear how the data helps inform decisions. In some cases the process has the direct involvement of the senior management, while in other universities' action is realised through the committee structure. In some cases, where student unions are a major factor in decision-making, such as at Lund University, they play a significant role in the utilisation of the student feedback for improvement (Torper, 1997).

Feedback to students about outcomes of surveys is recognised as an important element (Williams and Cappuccini-Ansfield, 2007) but is not always carried out effectively, nor does it always produce the awareness intended. Some institutions utilise current lines of communication between tutors and students or feed back through the student unions and student representatives. All of these forms depend upon the effectiveness of these lines of communication. Other forms of feedback used include articles in university magazines, posters and summaries aimed at students. The satisfaction approach developed at UCE, and adopted widely, provided a basis for internal improvement in a top-down/bottom-up process. At UCE, it involved the vice-chancellor, deans and directors of services. There was a well-developed analysis, reporting, action and feedback cycle. The results of the student feedback questionnaire were reported to the level of faculty and programme. The report was written in an easily accessible style, combining satisfaction and importance ratings that clearly showed areas of excellence and areas for improvement. The report was published (with an ISBN number) and was available in hard copy and on a public website. The action that followed the survey was reported back to the students through an annual publication. The approach worked, as the level of student satisfaction improved over a period stretching back nearly two decades (Kane et al., 2008).

Institutions that have used and adapted the UCE model include Sheffield Hallam University, Glamorgan University, Cardiff Institute of Higher Education (now University of Wales Institute, Cardiff), Buckingham College of Higher Education (now Buckinghamshire New University), University of Greenwich and University of Central Lancashire as well as overseas institutions such as Auckland University of Technology (New Zealand), Lund University (Sweden), City University (Hong Kong) and Jagiellonian University (Poland). All of these institutions have a similar approach, collecting student views to input into management decision-making. Where they varied is in the degree to which they made the findings public and produced reports for students outlining actions that have resulted from the survey.

When developing an institution-wide survey it is recommended that:

- They should provide both data for internal improvement and information for external stakeholders, therefore the results and subsequent action should be published.

- If the improvement function is to be effective, it is first necessary to establish an action cycle that clearly identifies lines of responsibility and feedback.

- Surveys need to be tailored to fit the improvement needs of the institution. Making use of stakeholder inputs (especially those of students) in the design of questionnaires is a useful process in making the survey relevant. System-wide generic questions are of little value.

- Only information that will be acted upon is collected.

- Importance as well as satisfaction ratings are recommended as this provides key indicators of what students regard as crucial in their experience and thus enables a clear action focus.

- For improvement purposes, reporting needs to be to the level at which effective action can be implemented; for example, programme organisation needs to be reported to the level of programmes, computing facilities to the level of faculties, learning resources to the level of libraries.

- Reports need to be written in an accessible style: rather than tables densely packed with statistics, data should be converted to a simple grading that incorporates satisfaction and importance scores, where the latter are used, thus making it easy for readers to identify areas of excellence and areas for improvement.

Faculty-level satisfaction with provision

Faculty-level surveys (based on pre-coded questionnaires) are similar to those undertaken at institution level. They tend to focus only on those aspects of the experience that the faculty controls or can directly influence. They often tend to be an unsatisfactory combination of general satisfaction with facilities and an attempt to gather information on satisfaction with specific learning situations. In most cases, these surveys are an additional task for faculty administrators; they are often based on an idiosyncratic set of questions and tend not to be well analysed, if at all. They are rarely linked into a meaningful improvement action cycle.

Where there is an institution-wide survey, disaggregated and reported to faculty level, faculty-based surveys tend to be redundant. Where faculty surveys overlap with institutional ones, there is often dissonance that affects response rates.

Faculty-level surveys are not really necessary, if well-structured institution-wide surveys are in place. If faculty-level surveys are undertaken it is recommended that:

- they do not clash with or repeat elements of existing institution-wide surveys;
- where both coexist, it is probably better to attempt to collect faculty data through qualitative means, focusing on faculty-specific issues untouched by institution-wide surveys;
- they are properly analysed and linked into a faculty-level action and feedback cycle, otherwise cynicism will rapidly manifest itself and undermine the credibility of the whole process.

Programme-level satisfaction with the learning and teaching

Programme-level surveys are not always based on questionnaires, although most tend to be. In some cases, feedback on programmes is solicited through qualitative discussion sessions, which are minuted. These may make use of focus groups. Informal feedback on programmes is a continuous part of the dialogue between students and lecturers. As identified above, informal feedback is an important source of information for improvement at this level. However, as Jones (2003) noted:

What is receiving less attention, and stands to be eclipsed as a means of measuring quality, are traditional quality assurance measures, administered by academics at the micro (delivery) level both as ongoing continuous improvement in response to verbal feedback from students, and in response to periodic, often richly qualitative, feedback from students on completion of a particular course of study. (p. 24)

James and McInnis (1997) had also shown that 'Less structured evaluation through informal discussion between staff and students was also considered an important means of receiving feedback on student satisfaction in most programmes' (p. 107).

Programme-level surveys tend to focus on the teaching and learning, course organisation and programme-specific learning resources. However, in a modularised environment, programme-level analysis of the learning situation tends to be 'averaged' and does not necessarily provide clear indicators of potential improvement of the programme without further enquiry at the module level. The link into any action is far from apparent in many cases. Where a faculty undertakes a survey of all its programmes of this type, there may be mechanisms, in theory, to encourage action but, in practice, the time lag involved in processing the questionnaires by hard-pressed faculty administrators tends to result in little timely improvement following the feedback.

In a modularised environment, where modular-level feedback is encouraged (see below), there is less need for programme-level questionnaire surveys. Where the institution-wide survey is comprehensive and disaggregates to the level of programmes, there is also a degree of redundancy in programme-level surveys. Again, if programme-level and institutional-level run in parallel there is a danger of dissonance.

Programme questionnaires are particularly common for final-year students coming to the end of their studies, who are asked to reflect back on the whole degree. The standardised programme evaluation approach reached its nadir in Australia with the development of the Course Evaluation Questionnaire (CEQ). This was a national minimalist survey aimed at graduates of Australian higher education institutions. The cost benefit of the CEQ has been a continuing area of debate in Australia.

Programme-level questionnaire surveys are probably not necessary if the institution has both a well-structured institution-wide survey, reporting to programme level, and structured module-level feedback. If programme-level surveys are undertaken it is recommended that:

- they do not clash with institution-wide surveys or module-level feedback if they exist;
- where programme-level information is needed for improvement purposes, it is probably better to obtain qualitative feedback on particular issues through discussion sessions or focus groups;
- they must be properly analysed and linked into a programme-level action and feedback cycle.

Module-level feedback

Feedback on specific modules or units of study provides an important element of continuous improvement. The feedback tends to focus on the specific learning and teaching associated with the module, along with some indication of the problems of accessing module-specific learning resources. Module-level feedback, both formal and informal, involves direct or mediated feedback from students to teachers about the learning situation within the module or unit of study.

The primary form of feedback at this level is direct informal feedback via dialogue. However, although this feedback may often be acted upon, it is rarely evident in any accounts of improvements based on student feedback. It constitutes the most important form of feedback in that it is probably the most effective spur to action on the part of receptive and conscientious academics in the development of the teaching and learning situation. Not all teachers are receptive to informal feedback and arrogant or indifferent lecturers can be found, in all institutions, who only hear what they want to hear and treat student views with indifference.

In most institutions, there is a requirement for some type of formal collection and reporting of module-level feedback, usually to be included in programme annual reports. Some institutions do not specify a particular data collection process and the lecturers decide on the appropriate method for the formal collection of feedback. Increasingly, though, institutions are imposing formal questionnaire templates, using online data collection methods; often with very low response rates, which provides another excuse for lecturers and managers to ignore the results (Douglas and Douglas, 2006).

Module-level questionnaire feedback is often superficial, generating satisfactory answers to teacher performance questions in the main. This results in little information on what would improve the learning situation and, because of questionnaire-processing delays, rarely benefits the students who provide the feedback. The use of questionnaires tends to inhibit qualitative discussion at the unit level. As Lomas and Nicholls (2005) pointed out, much of the evaluation of teaching rests largely on student feedback and often individuals within departments 'become objects of that evaluation, rather than participants within the process' (p. 139).

Direct, qualitative feedback is far more useful in improving the learning situation within a module of study. Qualitative discussion between staff (or facilitators) and students about the content and approach in particular course units or modules provides a rapid and in-depth appreciation of positive and negative aspects of taught modules. If written feedback is required, open questions on questionnaires are used that encourage students to say what would constitute an improvement for them, rather than rating items on a schedule drawn up by a teacher or, worse, an administrator.

However, qualitative feedback is sometimes seen as more time-consuming to arrange and analyse and, therefore, as constituting a less popular choice than handing out questionnaires or asking students to complete an online survey. Where compliance overshadows motivated improvement, recourse to questionnaires is likely.

In many instances, questionnaires used for module-level feedback are not analysed properly or in a timely fashion unless controlled by a central bureaucratic unit. Although most institutions insist on the collection of module-level data, the full cycle of analysis, reporting, action and feedback to originators of the data rarely occurs.

Module-level feedback is vital for the ongoing evolution of modules and the teaching team need to be responsive to both formal and informal feedback. It is, therefore, recommended that feedback systems at the module level:

- should include both formal and informal feedback;
- should complement institution-wide surveys, which cannot realistically report to module level;
- should be tailored to the improvement and development needs of the module (and therefore 'owned' by the module team), which obviates the need for standardised, institution-wide, module-level questionnaires that intimate compliance and accountability rather than improvement;
- must ensure appropriate analysis of the data and link into a module-level action and feedback cycle;
- do not need to be reported externally but should form part of internal programme reviews.

Appraisal of teacher performance by students

Some institutions focus on the performance of teaching staff rather than wider aspects of student satisfaction. Ewell (1993) noted projects being conducted by, *inter alia*, Astin and Pace in the USA, where feedback questionnaires played a considerable part in the appraisal of academics' performance. As a result of government pressure in the 1990s, institutions in the UK went through a period of collecting student views on the performance of particular teachers, known as 'teacher assessment'. Marsh and Roche (1993) developed the Students Evaluations of Educational Quality (SEEQ) instrument, designed to provide both diagnostic feedback to faculty that will be useful for the improvement of teaching and to provide a measure of teaching effectiveness to be used in personnel and administrative decision-making. Many institutions around the world use, or have used, standardised surveys of student appraisal of teaching, especially where there are a lot of part-time teachers (for example, at the London School of Economics, UK and Tuiuti University, Parana, Brazil).

The use of student evaluations of teacher performance is sometimes part of a broader peer and self-assessment approach to teaching quality. In some cases, they are used as part of the individual review of staff and can be taken into account in promotion and tenure situations, which was the case at Wellington and Otago Universities in New Zealand and in many institutions in the United States.

Teacher-appraisal surveys may provide some inter-programme comparison of teacher performance. However, standardised teacher-appraisal questionnaires tend, in practice, to focus on a limited range of areas and rarely address the development of student learning. Often, the standardised form is a bland compromise designed by managers or a committee that serves nobody's purposes. They are often referred to by the derogatory label of 'happy forms', as they are usually a set of questions about the reliability, enthusiasm, knowledge, encouragement and communication skills of named lecturers. Student appraisal of teachers tends to be a blunt instrument. Depending on the questions and the analysis, it has the potential to identify very poor teaching but, in the main, the results give little indication of how things can be improved. Appraisal forms are rarely of much use for incremental and continuous improvement.

In the vast majority of cases, there is no feedback at all to students about outcomes. Views on individual teacher performance are usually deemed confidential and subject to closed performance-review or development interviews with a senior manager. Hence, there is no opportunity to close the loop. At Auckland University, for example, the Student Evaluation of Courses and Teaching (SECAT) process was managed by the lecturers themselves and the results only passed on to managers in staff development interviews if the lecturer wanted to. Copenhagen Business School is a rare example of an institution that, in the 1990s, published the results within the institution.

Students' appraisal of teacher performance has a limited function, which, in practice, is ritualistic rather than improvement-oriented. Any severe problems are usually identified quickly via this mechanism. Repeated use leads to annoyance and cynicism on the part of students and teachers. Students become disenchanted because they rarely receive any feedback on the views they have offered. Lecturers become cynical and annoyed because they see student appraisal of teaching as a controlling rather than improvement-oriented tool. Thus, it is recommended that:

- use of student appraisal of teaching should be sparing;
- if used, avoid endlessly repeating the process;
- if used, ask questions about the student learning as well as the teacher performance;
- ensure that action is taken, and seen to be taken, to resolve and monitor the problems that such appraisals identify;
- only report outcomes as necessary to ensure improvement.

Multiple surveys: cosmetic or inclusive?

Institutions often have a mixture of the different types of student feedback, to which might be added graduate and employer surveys. The information gathered is, far too often, simply that – information. There are many circumstances when nothing is done with the information. It is not used to effect changes. Often it is not even collected with a use in mind. Perhaps, far too often, it is a cosmetic exercise.

There is more to student feedback than collecting data and the following are important issues. If collecting student views, only collect what can be made use of. It is counterproductive to ask students for information and then not use it. Students become cynical and unco-operative if they think no one really cares about what they think. It is important to heed, examine and make use of student views, whether provided formally or informally. However, if data from surveys of students is going to be useful, then it needs to be transformed into meaningful, clearly reported, information that can be used at the appropriate level to guide improvement. It is important to ensure that action takes place on the basis of student views and that *action is seen to take place*. This requires clear lines of communication, so that the impact of student views is fed back to students. In short, there needs to be a line of accountability back to the students to close the circle, whether that be at the institution or module level. It is not sufficient that students find out indirectly, if at all, that they have had a role in institutional policy.

Qualitative feedback is far more valuable and nuanced for improvement purposes than responses from standardised quantitative questionnaires. Jones (2003) argued that it is a mistake for institutional managers and central administrators to rely on formal survey data.

> Furthermore, there is often rich qualitative feedback (both formal and informal) collected at the decentralised educational delivery point that it is not easy to summarise for use at a central level . . . Without this rich depth of feedback, centrally administered quantitative surveys often distort student feedback. What is then required is a means to link the two levels and forms of student feedback as part of a holistic quality assessment. (p. 225)

Williams and Cappuccini-Ansfield (2007) also made it clear, in their seminal paper, that relying on national surveys is inadequate for improvement purposes. Comparing the UK generic national student survey (NSS) and, for example, the tailored approach embodied in the Student Satisfaction Survey (SSS) approach (Harvey et al., 1997) that reflects the specific circumstances and issues in an institution, they noted that:

> the two are very different survey instruments, created for different purposes and should be used accordingly. The NSS is designed as a broad brush instrument, short and simple, which aims to measure the concept of quality, using a single format that can be used at all higher education institutions. The SSS, in contrast, is a detailed instrument, which aims to measure satisfaction with all aspects of the student experience and is tailored specifically to the needs of students at a particular institution. The SSS is specifically designed to be central to internal continuous quality improvement processes, whereas the NSS cannot be effectively used for this purpose . . .

There are dangers with the nation-wide league table approach enabled by the NSS that only the minimum information, in this case, mean scores, is used to make crude comparisons between the value for money of very different institutions. The SSS helps to address an individual institution's accountability by involving students in the quality process, both by giving feedback to them and responding to feedback from them. There is value in using surveys to provide information about institutions for prospective students, but there are potential problems with making fair comparisons between institutions. (p. 170)

They also pointed out that 'final-year students filling in the national survey may give favourable scores if they want their degree from that institution to be valued' (Williams and Cappuccini-Ansfield, 2007: 171). Indeed, there were cases in the UK of staff attempting to manipulate students to give high ratings so that the institution would appear higher on the league tables (Attwood, 2008; Mostrous, 2008; Furedi, 2008; Swain, 2009).

Williams and Cappuccini-Ansfield also highlighted the danger that NSS data 'will be used simplistically, without a great deal of thought to how well it represents the quality of education offered by the institution'. Further, 'Its administration can interfere with each institution's important internal quality processes and most certainly can never replace them' (Williams and Cappuccini-Ansfield, 2007: 171).

The recent British Parliamentary Select Committee reviewing higher education also remarked on the limitations of the NSS.

101. **We accept that the National Student Survey is a good starting point but caution against an over-reliance on it.** The University of Hertfordshire said that there was 'a significant tension' with the National Student Survey being a tool for improvement and also used in league tables. It noted that there were 'documented instances of abuse (and probably an additional unknown amount of this activity that is undetected) because moving higher in the league tables might be deemed more important than getting students to reflect fairly on their experience of an institution as part of an enhancement exercise'. We noted two instances where it was suggested that universities may be encouraging students filling in the Survey to be positive about the institution. (House of Commons, 2009, para. 101)

Feedback to students

As well as feedback *from* students on their learning environment, it is important to provide students with feedback on their work and learning. This is different from completing the feedback loop, which is primarily about providing students with information on action that results from their feedback. Feedback *to* students on their work and the progress of their learning refers to the commentary that accompanies summative gradings or that guides students through formative assessment. In the United Kingdom, the Quality Assurance Agency's (2009) *Code of Practice*, Part 6, refers to the assessment of students. Precept 12 of Part 6 of the Code states that: 'Institutions should ensure that appropriate feedback is provided to students on assessed work in a way that promotes learning and facilitates improvement.'

Feedback to students on their learning and feedback from students on their experience are treated quite separately in many settings, when, in fact, there is potential for symbiosis. Feedback to students on the work they have done, if provided appropriately, helps them improve, gives them an idea of how they are progressing, aids motivation and empowers them as learners. Badly done, feedback to students can be confusing, misleading, demotivating and disempowering.

As long as feedback from students is perceived as some kind of consumer satisfaction, rather than as integral to a transformative learning context, feedback from students will be disengaged from feedback to students.

Before examining the symbiosis, there are a few observations on appropriate feedback to students on their learning. Feedback should be informative, which requires understandable explanations that are unambiguous and clear and not an exhibition of the tutor's erudition. Students may not be as familiar with academic language, concepts and nuances as the lecturer may assume. Feedback should be structured, focused and consistent, as well as providing appropriate indications of relative progress. Importantly, for students, feedback needs to be provided promptly, closely following the hand-in date or event. Where the organisational structure makes this difficult, early feedback to the whole class on key points can be a valuable stopgap.

It is essential that feedback on assessed work clearly indicates how to improve, by providing specific detail on any misapprehensions in the student's work and by making helpful suggestions on improvement of both particulars and of written or oral presentation style. Feedback sessions, of whatever type, need to be positive experiences even where there is bad news. Feedback on work should enhance self-esteem, not damage it; and so tutors need to be aware of the impact of their feedback and to be sure they take into account the wider context of the students' lives.

Typical unhelpful feedback includes work that is returned with just a summative grade or comment, or is annotated with ticks and crosses but no commentary or explanation. Vague, general or confusing remarks, such as 'explain', 'deconstruct' or 'isn't this contentious?' are unhelpful, as are subjective or idiosyncratic remarks, such as 'Weber's analysis is fatuous'.

The UK Parliamentary Select Committee report stated:

> We note that the QAA produced a code of practice on the assessment of students . . . We are therefore surprised that feedback on students' work is an issue of such concern . . . **It is our view that, whether at the level of module, course, department or institution, students should be provided with more personalised information about the intended parameters of their own assessment experience. It is unacceptable and disheartening for any piece of work whether good, average or poor to be returned to a student with only a percentage mark and no comments or with feedback but after such a long time that the feedback is ineffective.** (House of Commons, 2009: 85–6, emphasis in original)

The Committee thus concluded with a recommendation to Government to ensure a 'code of practice on (i) the timing, (ii) the quantity, and (iii) the format and content of feedback and require higher education institutions to demonstrate how they are following the Code when providing feedback to students in receipt of support from the taxpayer' (House of Commons, 2009: 86–7).

Skilled feedback is not something that comes naturally; it is a tricky interpersonal relationship and staff need to spend time developing feedback skills. In an attempt to improve feedback, the University of Cambridge, Department of Plant Sciences (2008), for example, used focus groups and questionnaires to examine student perceptions and found that many students thought they were not provided with enough useful feedback to help them improve. This concern was mirrored by supervisors, who felt unsure about how to provide effective formative feedback. The result was a workshop in which supervisors reviewed a list of comments made on different essays for the same student. They discussed the effectiveness of the different marking styles, which ranged from directive comments to just ticks and marks. Supervisors were also asked to examine a variety of exemplar essays that had all been awarded an upper-second grade and to discuss what would be worth commenting on, the strengths and weaknesses of the work, and how the essays could be improved. Such processes greatly enhance the efficacy of the process of feedback on student work.

All this suggests the importance of one-to-one feedback tutorials with student and staff. Ideally these should be face-to-face, but they might also be conducted virtually. Getting students to undertake a self-evaluation of the work they have undertaken, prior to a tutorial, is a useful way to explore how the student's self-perception relates to the tutor assessment.

In essence, feedback to students should be empowering. It should result in tutor and student agreeing what is to be done to improve; enabling students to evaluate their own performance and diagnose their own strengths and weaknesses. This, incidentally, is aided by developing reflective skills in the curriculum so that students are themselves well prepared and motivated to make effective use of the feedback that is available. Naidoo (2005), in discussing the Student Satisfaction approach, argued that: 'quality empowerment entails the concept of agency – the ability not only to participate in but also to shape education. Empowered students have the ability not only to make the correct choices with regard to institutions and programmes, but also to play a positive role in promoting and enhancing quality of education processes and outcomes' (p. 2).

Integrating feedback

Some of the most important criteria for quality, as specified by staff and students are: feedback on assessed work; fair assessment regimes; and clear assessment criteria. Feedback from students for continuous improvement processes should mesh with the processes for feedback to students about academic performance. However, as institutions collect more information from students about the service they receive, there is evidence of less formative feedback to students about their own academic, professional and intellectual development. This is in part because individual interaction between tutor and student is decreasing, or in some systems continues to be virtually non-existent.

There are ways to ensure a symbiosis between feedback from and feedback to students but this requires two things: a commitment to enabling learning; and recognition that feedback from students is not a consumerist reaction but integral to their own transformative learning. Thus, it is vital to ensure that feedback from students is about their learning and skill development rather than the performance of teachers. It is also important to create space for discussion tutorials in which both student perception of their learning experience and staff evaluation of the student's progress are openly discussed without prejudice. This will not only change the emphasis on learning (away from lectures, for example) but also implies a shift in the balance of power in the learning relationship. A critical dialogue replaces a unidirectional exertion of intellectual dominance.

Conclusions

Student feedback on their learning is one of the most effective tools in the ongoing improvement of the quality of higher education. It is not the only tool and should never be used as the only source of evidence in making changes. However, it is potentially a powerful force in guiding improvement, providing the data collection and analysis is effective, addresses the important issues, engages with the student learning experience and is acted upon in a timely manner.

Students are key stakeholders in the quality monitoring and assessment processes and it is important to obtain their views. However, as James and McInnis (1997) argued over a decade ago, one should have 'multiple strategies for student feedback' (p. 105). It is crucial to attach significance to informal feedback and not be beguiled by formal feedback mechanisms, which in the main are limited and lack fine distinction.

Far too many approaches to student feedback start by designing a questionnaire rather than exploring the purpose of student feedback. The consumerist view predominates in such method-led approaches, which, in the main, merely act as a public relations exercise or an indicator of accountability rather than as a real engagement with the student perspective. A clear analysis of the purpose and use of student feedback, a structure for implementing and communicating changes designed to improve the student learning experience, as well as a clear linkage between feedback from and feedback to students on their learning and progress, are essential if student feedback is to be more than a cosmetic exercise.

Notes

1. Since the change of name (and senior management team) the uniqueness of the UCE approach and the enormous value that it had for the university has been lost.

2. In some institutions programmes of study are referred to as 'courses' or 'pathways'. However, 'course' is a term used in some institutions to mean 'module' or 'unit' of study, that is, a sub-element of a programme of study. Due to the ambiguity of 'course', the terms 'programme of study' and 'module' will be used in this chapter.

References

Astin, A.W. (1982). 'Why not try some new ways of measuring quality?' *Educational Record*, 63(2), 10–15.

Attwood, R. (2008). 'Probe ordered into "manipulation"', *Times Higher Education*, 28 February 2008. Available online at: *http://www.timeshighereducation.co.uk/story.asp?sectioncode=26andstorycode=400809* (accessed 5 January 2010).

Ballantyne, C. (1997). 'Improving university teaching: giving feedback to students', in R. Pospisil and L. Willcoxson. (eds), *Learning Through Teaching, Proceedings of the 6th Annual Teaching Learning Forum*, pp. 12–15. Perth: Murdoch University.

Baxter, P.E. (1991). 'The TEVAL experience 1983–1988: the impact of a student evaluation of teaching scheme on university teachers', *Studies in Higher Education*, 16, 151–78.

Carr, S., Hamilton, E. and Meade, P. (2005). 'Is it possible? Investigating the influence of external quality audit on university performance', *Quality in Higher Education*, 11(3), 195–21.

Church, F. (2008). 'Students as consumers: the importance of student feedback in the quality assurance process', The UK Centre for Legal Education. Available online at: *http://www.ukcle.ac.uk/interact/lili/2001/church.html* (accessed 10 January 2010).

Douglas, J. and Douglas, A. (2006). 'Evaluating teaching quality', *Quality in Higher Education*, 12(1), 3–13.

Ewell, P. (1993). *A preliminary study of the feasibility and utility for national policy of instructional 'good practice' indicators in undergraduate education.* Report prepared for the National Center for Education Statistics, mimeo (Boulder, CO: NCHEMS).

Furedi, F. (2008). 'iPod for their thoughts?' *Times Higher Education*, 29 May 2008. Available online at: *http://www.timeshighereducation.co.uk/story.asp?sectioncode=26&storycode=402162* (accessed 15 January 2010).

Harvey, L. (2001). 'Getting student satisfaction', *Guardian*, 27 November. Online. Available online at: *http://www.guardian.co.uk/education/2001/nov/27/students* (accessed 16 January 2010).

Harvey, L. and Associates (1997). *Student Satisfaction Manual.* Buckingham: Open University Press.

Hill, R. (1995). 'A European student perspective on quality', *Quality in Higher Education*, 1(1), 67–75.

Horsburgh, M. (1998). 'Quality monitoring in two institutions: a comparison', *Quality in Higher Education*, 4(2), 115.

House of Commons, Innovation, Universities, Science and Skills Committee (2009). *Students and Universities: Eleventh Report of Session 2008–09, Volume I*. London: The Stationery Office.

James, R. and McInnis, C. (1997). 'Coursework masters degrees and quality assurance: implicit and explicit factors at programme level', *Quality in Higher Education*, 3(2), 101–12.

Jones, S. (2003). 'Measuring the quality of higher education: linking teaching quality measures at the delivery level to administrative measures at the university level', *Quality in Higher Education*, 9(3), 223–29.

Kane, D., Williams, J. and Cappuccini-Ansfield, G. (2008). 'Student satisfaction surveys: the value in taking an historical perspective', *Quality in Higher Education*, 14(2), 135–55.

Leckey, J. and Neill, N. (2001). 'Quantifying quality: the importance of student feedback', *Quality in Higher Education*, 7(1), 19–32.

Lomas, L. and Nicholls, G. (2005). 'Enhancing teaching quality through peer review of teaching', *Quality in Higher Education*, 11(2), 137–49.

Marsh, H.W. and Roche, L. (1993). 'The use of students' evaluations and an individually structured intervention to enhance university teaching effectiveness', *American Educational Research Journal*, 30, 217–51.

Massy, W.F. and French, N.J. (2001). 'Teaching and Learning Quality Process Review: what the programme has achieved in Hong Kong', *Quality in Higher Education*, 7(1), 33–45.

Mazelan, P., Brannigan, C., Green, D. and Tormey, P. (1992). *Report on the 1992 Survey of Student Satisfaction with their Educational Experience at UCE*. Birmingham: Student Satisfaction Research Unit, University of Central England.

Mostrous, A. (2008). 'Kingston University students told to lie to boost college's rank in government poll', *The Times*, 14 May 2008. Available online at: *http://www.timesonline.co.uk/tol/news/uk/article3924417.ece* (accessed 15 January 2010).

Naidoo, P. (2005). *Student Literacy and Empowerment*. Online. Available at: *http://www.che.ac.za/documents/d000110/Student_Quality_Literacy_Naidoo_2005.pdf* (accessed 16 January 2010).

Palermo, J. (2004). 'Closing the loop on student evaluations'. Available onlilne at: *http://www.aair.org.au/jir/2004Papers/PALERMO.pdf* (accessed 16 January 2010).

Powney, J. and Hall, S. (1998). *Closing the loop: the impact of student feedback on students' subsequent learning*. Edinburgh: Scottish Council for Research in Education.

Quality Assurance Agency for Higher Education (QAA) (2009). *Code of Practice*. Available online at: *http://www.qaa.ac.uk/academicinfrastructure/codeOfPractice/default.asp* (accessed 15 January 2010).

Rowley, J. (1996). 'Measuring quality in higher education', *Quality in Higher Education*, 2(3), 237–55.

Swain, H. (2009). 'A hotchpotch of subjectivity: the National Student Survey was a key indicator in the Guardian's university league tables. But is it fair?' *The Guardian*, 19 May 2009.

Torper, U. (1997). *Studentbarometern, Resultatredovisning* [The Student Barometer, Documentation of Results] Report No. 97:200. Lund: Lunds Universitet, Utvärderingsenheten.

University of Cambridge, Department of Plant Sciences (2008). *Feedback to students in the Department of Plant Sciences*. Report. Available online at: *http://www.admin.cam.ac.uk/offices/education/lts/lunch/lunch14.html* (accessed 16 January 2010).

Walker-Garvin, A. (undated). *Unsatisfactory Satisfaction: Student Feedback and Closing the Loop. Quality Promotion and Assurance*. Pietermaritzburg, South Africa: University of KwaZulu-Natal.

Watson, S. (2003). 'Closing the feedback loop: ensuring effective action from student feedback', *Tertiary Education and Management*, 9, 145–57.

Williams, J. (2002). 'Student satisfaction: a British model of effective use of student feedback in quality assurance and enhancement'. Paper presented at the *14th International Conference on assessment and Quality in Higher Education*, Vienna, 24–27 July.

Williams, J. and Cappuccini-Ansfield, G. (2007). 'Fitness for purpose? National and institutional approaches to publicising the student voice', *Quality in Higher Education*, 13(2), 159–72.

Yorke, M. (1995). 'Siamese Twins? Performance indicators in the service of accountability and enhancement', *Quality in Higher Education*, 1(1), 13–30.

Part 2
International perspectives

Student feedback in the US and global contexts

Fernando F. Padró

Abstract: Today's accountability processes for university performance require the use of student feedback for an increasing number of aspects of what universities do. This has to be done in a systematic way and made part of an institution's decision-making process. The challenge to the use of student feedback is the purpose behind the collection and analysis of this information. External stakeholders prefer the use of a customer-focused model in which what universities do is defined as a service. Academic staff and supporters of academe prefer an approach that recognises the traditional norms of academic performance. This chapter discusses the controversies, dilemmas and issues of using student feedback from the lens of evaluating the performance of academic units and staff in the USA, where the practice of generating student ratings is a long-standing one and where many of the concerns regarding the use of student feedback were initially raised.

Key words: institutional quality; meta-professional model; performance data; SERVQUAL; student feedback; student ratings; university accountability.

Introduction

St John, Kline and Asker (2001) wrote about the need to rethink the links between the funding of public higher education with accountability measures based on student-choice processes and student outcomes. Student outcomes are now considered the principal mechanism for determining successful performance of higher education institutions (HEIs). No longer are external reviews merely interested in the traditional input data; the focus is for input and throughput mechanisms to enhance and maximise student learning opportunities within the campus for traditional as well as the increasing number of non-traditional students. Description of programmes is not enough – universities have to know more about their product (Cronbach, 2000).

Student-choice processes place a greater emphasis on student-based information to identify needs in order to figure out how to better serve those needs. Student feedback is desirable because it helps determine student satisfaction with their interaction with the different elements of the university and measure the extent of active engagement by the students in terms of curricular and co-curricular programmes. The hope is that institutions will: (a) retain their students until graduation, (b) generate student learning that is attractive to potential employers or graduate programmes, and (c) enhance student loyalty as alumni to provide the university with funds, participative support, and feedback that allows the institution to provide a value-added experience while on campus and afterwards.

Traditional student information included in the application package (grades, entrance exams, personal information) provides only information specific to acceptance of students to HEIs and subsequent placement into residence halls, support programmes and/or courses (remedial, honours or advanced level). Grades alone are also insufficient to fully gauge student contentment with what they are getting out of their university experience. Thus, there is a need to know more about students and their satisfaction with their experience. From 1966 onward, the Cooperative Institutional Research Programme (CIRP), a national longitudinal study of the higher education system in the USA, has been regarded as a key source of comprehensive data on incoming and continuing students. An additional layer of student data has become available from 2000 onward through the National Survey of Student Engagement (NSSE), which annually documents on a national basis student participation in programmes and activities HEIs make available for learning and personal development. According to Kuh (2001), NSSE allows for the creation of national benchmarks of good practice for universities to use to measure their improvement efforts relative to academic concerns along with supportive campus environments.

The point of student feedback is to systematically use what had been collected informally for many years, such as information from alumni (cf. Braskamp and Ory, 1994), and formalise it so as to make it a meaningful component of institutional decision-making. This systematisation of data collection and the focus on incoming, current and former students (hopefully graduates) is shaped by the current reality of the nascent environment that Slaughter and Leslie (1997) called academic capitalism, an environment in which academic and professional staff have to navigate in more highly competitive situations driven by market-like behaviours.

Types of student feedback can be broken down into distinct categories (Table 2.1). Taken together, the model that emerges is a feedback process that has a striking resemblance to Brocato and Potocki's (1996) customer-based definition of student and quality of instruction in contrast to the more traditional notions of academic endeavour and quality:

- The student's education is the product.
- The customers for this product are the students, families, employers and other academic staff.
- The student definition of quality is that education which meets student expectations.

Quality focuses on two process-related questions: '*What is wanted?*' and '*How do we do it?*' (Straker, 2001). The inclusion and significance in the use of student feedback is an example of how quality management and assessment are more widely accepted today (Kitagawa, 2003), even if there are 'fundamental differences of view of the appropriate relationship that should be established between higher education institutions and their external evaluators' (European Association for Quality Assurance in Higher Education, 2005: 11). This is why the Malcolm Baldrige

Table 2.1 Different types of student feedback collected by HEIs

For student satisfaction purposes (Pate, 1993)	For service quality purposes (Lehtinen and Lehtinen, 1991; Pereda, Airey and Bennett, 2007)
■ Psychological wellness satisfaction ■ Job-type satisfaction ■ Consumer-type satisfaction	■ Physical quality – products and services: general services, teaching and learning facilities, accommodation ■ Interactive quality: academic instruction, guidance, interaction with staff and students ■ Corporate image: recognition, reputation, value for money

National Quality Award Education Criterion 3.1(b) 2 asks educational institutions how they:

> ... build and manage relationships with students and STAKEHOLDERS to
>
> ■ acquire new students and STAKEHOLDERS;
>
> ■ meet their requirements and exceed their expectations at each stage of their relationship with you; and
>
> ■ increase their ENGAGEMENT with the [institution]?
> (Baldrige National Quality Program, 2009: 13)

And although voluntary regional accrediting bodies in the USA have not fully adopted the Baldrige criteria as the blueprint for external reviews, one can see a more detailed tactic in the New England Association of Colleges and Universities (NEASC) (2006) standard 4.50:

> The institution uses a variety of quantitative and qualitative methods to understand the experiences and learning outcomes of its students. Inquiry may focus on a variety of perspectives, including understanding the process of learning, being able to describe student experiences and learning outcomes in normative terms, and gaining feedback from alumni, employers, and others situated to help in the description and assessment of student learning. The institution devotes appropriate attention to ensuring that its methods of understanding student learning are trustworthy and provide information useful in the continuing improvement of programs and services for students. (p. 12)

Student feedback in the evaluation of academic programmes and instruction

Student evaluation of courses or units and of instruction has been used at HEIs for many years. As far back as 1949, Guthrie asserted that teaching is best judged by students as well as by colleagues. Thus, in the USA, by 1994, 98 per cent of respondents indicated a systematic student evaluation of classroom teaching is occurring at their campuses, with the other 2 per cent indicating that their institutions are considering it (Glassick et al., 1997). In Australia, the Course Experience Questionnaire was fully implemented in 1993 and continues to be used to this day for the purpose of allowing for a comparison of programmes among Australia's universities. Meanwhile, especially under the re-engineering of higher education occurring in Europe under the Bologna Process, most European universities are instituting some sort of student evaluation of teaching – with the emphasis seeming to be in the form of student satisfaction (cf. Wiers-Jennsen et al. 2002).

The remainder of this chapter is dedicated to discussing relevant issues and concerns regarding student feedback within the framework of evaluating classroom instruction. To say that this is a controversial topic is an understatement. This is why Aleamoni's (1999) literature review discusses and then rebuts many of the myths surrounding the use of student feedback as a means of evaluating instruction and instructor performance. What will come through is the challenge of framing the process and use of student feedback in relation to the job performance of instructors. A continuum seems to be developing. One side is represented by Arreola et al.'s (2003) meta-professional model for faculty, while on the other side is the service quality instrument – SERVQUAL– which others have made applicable to higher education first developed by Parasumaran et al. (1985, 1988). The rationale behind SERVQUAL is to measure consumers' perceptions of quality when there is an absence of objective measures. This approach, as can be seen, easily aligns with many of the concepts driving the need for student feedback.

Case study

Seashoal Lows University (SLU) is a medium to large, urban comprehensive teaching-focused university of about 8,000 undergraduate and graduate students majoring in the arts and sciences and professional programmes in business, counseling psychology, education, and human and health services (a Master's Large Comprehensive institution under the current Carnegie Classification Index). It has been using student evaluations of its instructors for a number of years. However, the faculty senate, the faculty collective bargaining unit, and individual faculty have been complaining over the appropriateness of how this is used and the purpose behind it. Student evaluations of faculty (SEFs) are externally created instruments given either through paper and pencil instruments or online. These are given near the end of the academic term. Problematic to the faculty and its related university organisations is that these instruments have become the primary element in deciding faculty promotion and tenure. According to the Agreement faculty have with SLU, the review process should be based on a portfolio provided by the instructor going up for review that includes publications, conference presentations, external and internal funding awards (when applicable), course syllabi and materials, classroom observations by peers selected by the applicant and the administration, observations by the supervising administrator, student evaluation of faculty results, documentation of university and community service, and external reviews of the portfolio by individuals agreed to by the faculty member and the head of the academic unit. Decisions are made by a committee within the School, with recommendations given to the Dean who, in turn, makes a recommendation to the Provost and President.

There are two principal types of faculty: faculty who have asked to be considered for their research as well as instruction; and those who want to be primarily considered for promotion and tenure based on their instruction (with criteria ostensibly following the suggestions put forth by Ernest Boyer (1990) regarding the scholarship of teaching). Programme-level accreditation at times provides guidelines for promotion and tenure for certain programmes while the university's overall criteria are purposefully kept nebulous to avoid potential litigation from those denied promotion and/or tenure.

The issue is that in practice, the main point of evidence has become the student evaluation of the applicant when it comes to instruction. It has become apparent that committees and responsible administrators weigh student evaluations disproportionately when compared to course syllabi and materials or classroom observation by peers and administrators. Faculty complaints range from inappropriateness of the instrument, because it is not linked or validated to institutional norms of good teaching, to the belief that student feedback really represents a popularity contest because they may not be the best judge of content. Some also are concerned that the time when these are given ties student observations to their idea of what their grade should/will be and, moreover, there are complaints that there is no real instructional support for faculty because there is no formal capacity to assist faculty – especially junior faculty – in improving their instruction.

SLU's administration does not want to change the student evaluation process because they are concerned that the time and cost taken to create and validate an in-house instrument may adversely impact accreditation-related data analysis and reporting. They also like the idea that they can use the external instrument in order to compare instructor ratings with other institutions. Finally, the administrators believe that the external instrument is validated and, as a result, the instruments do provide an accurate evaluation of faculty, more so than the other factors that can be influenced through personalities and politics.

SLU realistically does not use the data collected for benchmark analysis although it can. It does not use the data collected for continuous improvement purposes or to at least check for problems with instruction. However, the University's administration is mindful of the change in the external regulatory environment that identifies with the student as a consumer and wants to maintain and enhance responsiveness to student needs and expectations. Therefore, there is an impasse within the institution. One side discounts the merit of student feedback and at best is resigned to have to live with it. The other side sees student feedback as a way of maintaining its regulatory compliance requirements and finds that its ability to quantify instruction provides a more compelling measure to make career decisions.

Issues

There are seven issues the scenario brings up:

- the role of student evaluation of instruction in staffing decisions (continuation, promotion, tenure) as distinguished from programme/ unit performance;
- the weight given to student feedback in staffing decisions;
- the appropriateness of instrument used to evaluate courses within a programme/unit and instruction;
- how the data are used for analysis purposes (institutional and individual performance);
- the decision-making processes used surrounding the creation, content, validation, administration and use of the instrument;
- the resources available to support improvement activities as a follow-up to data results;
- the need for a careful and clear link between HEI staffing decision-making processes and the role of student feedback (including contractual agreements between the university and collective bargaining unit).

These have to be considered as a whole rather than as separate components because these are all interrelated. Regardless of approach taken, whether it is from a more traditional professional development model or a customer service model, there are legal implications to consider along with fitness of purpose, morale and buy-in concerns from all university employees and students themselves. Employees are concerned about job security and fairness. At play are the strategies individuals use as part of their sense-making process to determine what is needed for them to succeed at the HEI (cf. Weick, 1995). Apart from these aspects, it is important not to forget that students pay attention to the extent their information is actually considered and followed-up on, which in turn impacts their future engagement.

Probably the most important consideration is to identify and clearly articulate the reasons for and use of student feedback on instruction. For example, the American Council on Education and the American Association of University Professors (2000) jointly agree that stated criteria for tenure apply in actual practice. The extent to which these instruments are used for hiring/firing and promotion purposes may differ throughout the world. In many countries, feedback instruments are strictly utilised to measure institutional performance of academic units. Nevertheless, if the data reflect weakness at the individual level, individuals can be identified to receive additional support. Anecdotally, some HEIs identify the bottom 10 per cent of performers to give them training to improve their instruction.

The evaluation of academic staff performance reflects the role they play at their particular campus. Traditionally, the roles are divided into the triad of research, instruction and service, often in this order of importance. The roles of academic staff at a particular institution ought to be clearly defined and understood. It helps to know the criteria or standards for continuity and promotion. Review mechanisms and feedback have to be linked to these criteria or standards. Techniques and instruments need to be reliable and show practical and/or statistical validity. Techniques and instruments have to be weighted as part of the codification of value process relative to specific performance (Arreola, 2007). Techniques and instruments have the challenge of needing to overcome, as much as possible and feasible, Birnbaum's (1988) characteristics of an anarchic university (unclear goals, imprecise technology, fluid participation, and solutions looking for problems). And, in addition, there should be an institutional support element at the campus-wide or unit level such as a centre of teaching and learning (cf. Padró, 2010; Institutional Management in Higher Education, 2007) to ensure improvement either in remedial or enhancement modes.

Two questions of role and use of student feedback in the area of instruction emerge, the one area of the triad where they are in a position to provide useful observations. The first question is: *What is the role of student evaluations of instruction? Formative – focusing on diagnostics and continuous improvement – or summative in scope leading toward staffing decisions?* Pallett's (2006) observations provide an answer:

> Regrettably, the diagnostic value of student ratings is often not realized, even though many faculty developers and teaching improvement specialists attest to their potential. There are at least three reasons for this. First, there is so much emphasis on the summative component of student ratings . . . that what can be learned to improve teaching is often overlooked . . . Second, useful, valid and reliable student ratings forms are difficult to create. This is especially true in developing a form that can truly support improvement efforts. Third, for real gains in teaching skills to occur, support and mentoring needs to be provided. While those making personnel assessments should not be precluded from guiding improvement efforts, others not involved in the evaluation process also need to be available. (pp. 51–52)

The second question is: *What is the best type of instrument for students to use in giving feedback about courses and instruction?* There are three approaches. The first one is for an HEI to develop its own instrument. This requires careful construction based on the institutional values of teaching, followed by appropriate reliability and validity studies that can take a few years to complete. Arreola (2007) described a ten-phase process for creating these forms:

Phase 1:   Determine the issues to be measured by the form.
Phase 2:   Write or select the items.
Phase 3:   Develop appropriate response scales.
Phase 4:   Conduct field trials to gather the data needed for subsequent validity and reliability determination.
Phase 5:   Conduct a factor analytic study.
Phase 6:   Develop subscales based on the result of the factor analysis.
Phase 7:   Refine the form.
Phase 8:   Establish norms.
Phase 9:   Organize the items.
Phase 10:   Implement the student rating system. (pp. 114–116)

Braskamp and Ory (1994) classify common forms of assessment of academic staff into three categories:

- Omnibus form: fixed set of items, administered to students or participants in all classes, workshops, etc. given by the HEI;
- Goal-based form: students rate their own performance or progress on stated course goals and objectives; currently, learner outcomes;
- Cafeteria system: bank of items from which academic staff can select those considered most relevant for assessing one's own course.

This typology suggests HEIs carefully consider the options available under this action plan. Regardless of type, without paying attention to the reliability and validity part of the process, questions arise regarding how good the data are and their usefulness. In addition, if staffing considerations are proved to be significantly impacted by this instrument, then there may be tortuous litigation ahead.

The second approach to utilising student feedback instruments is to use commercially available or 'off-the-shelf' forms created and sold by a private firm. This is the track represented in the case study.

Arreola (2007) does indicate that it may be a good idea to consider adopting or adapting a professionally-developed form because many locally-generated student feedback forms may not possess the necessary psychometric qualities of reliability and validity. These instruments have already been tested for reliability and validity. In addition, the use of such instruments allows for national comparisons between comparable institutions using that particular survey. Comparative data can be used for improvement reasons, personnel grounds and marketing/rating data that students and parents can use in making choices on which university to attend, and documenting performance of programmes and units as part of benchmarking exercises. A key aspect to deciding on whether or which instrument to select is to determine which one provides the university data that are meaningful to it based on how the data will be utilised.

Critics of using these commercial instruments have numerous concerns, ranging from appropriateness of the concept of student feedback itself to alignment of items/questions to institutional normative references of instruction to how data are interpreted and subsequently used. Some of these concerns echo what detractors think about home-grown forms. Ramsden's (1991) research using the literature review by Marsh (1987) and others makes the case for an association between student learning and student perception of teaching. Aleamoni (1999) takes a look at these characteristic arguments against the use of student feedback from the lens of studies looking at these issues. What Aleamoni found was that most of the contentions do not hold based on available findings. For example, he countered the complaint that 'Students cannot make consistent judgments about the instructor because of their immaturity, lack of experience, and capriciousness' with evidence dating as far back as 1924 indicating just the opposite. 'The stability of student ratings from one year to the next resulted in substantial correlations in the range of 0.87 to 0.89' (p. 153). Aleamoni also countered another typical complaint, that 'Student rating forms are both unreliable and invalid', by arguing that '[W]ell-developed instruments and procedures for their administration can yield high internal consistency reliabilities . . . in the 0.90 range' while the vast majority of studies regarding instrument validity indicated the 'existence of moderate to high positive correlations' (p. 155).

The third approach toward what student feedback instrument(s) to use may not be a choice at all, because institutions are to use or adapt a national instrument required by national protocols or a national quality assurance process (cf. Institutional Management in Higher Education, 2007). The example in mind is the course experience questionnaire utilised in Australia, an approach the popularity of which is expanding to other countries, reflecting Ewell's (2002) observation that assessment and accountability have become entwined. Linking accountability with the assessment of learning means, at one level, a change in the conceptual paradigm of assessment from an evaluative stance to that of assuming active and collective responsibility for learning while, at another level, it suggests the evolving of a learning organisation. The basis for this thinking is using a national instrument as part of a quality teaching framework in which students play a formal role, as is evolving in Europe (ENQA, 2005) and elsewhere in countries establishing their own national quality assurance system. According to the OECD:

> Students can collaborate with teachers and leaders in the definition of the initiative (and of the quality teaching concept itself), keeping the interaction alive and raising concerns about teaching, learning environments, quality of content and teacher attitudes. They can best contribute if invited to serve on governing bodies or used as evaluation experts on par with academic reviewers. (Institutional Management in Higher Education, 2007: 75)

In reviewing the literature and practices surrounding the use of student feedback for quality assurance purposes in the area of instructional performance of individuals, units and whole HEIs, what becomes apparent is that there is a continuum developing. One extreme emphasises professional development based on carefully structured multiple processes with adequate support mechanisms that help individuals succeed in their roles within the triad of research, instruction, and service. The other extreme is a strict customer service model based on documenting performance in instruction for institutional success, utilising comparative analyses so that different stakeholders can use this decision for informed decision-making (e.g. personal choice of institution, national policy determination of success and alignment to national intellectual/human capital needs). Below is a discussion of the models that exemplify the two extremes of the continuum.

The meta-profession model of faculty

'Faculty performance is complex and dynamic' (Braskamp and Ory, 1994: 22). Its evaluation should reflect the complexity of faculty work framed within clearly communicated institutional goals and expectations. The meta-profession model is selected as a highly systematised approach toward the evaluation of faculty that reflects these points. What this perspective represents is a review process that maintains the traditional focus of evaluating academic staff using the broader brushstrokes of competencies that cannot be defined only in terms of customer satisfaction.

Arreola et al. (2003) extended Boyer's (1990) effort at making the professoriate and others rethink the role of academic staff at universities. Currently, academic staff 'must perform at a professional level in a variety of roles that require expertise and skills in areas that often extend beyond the faculty member's specific area of scholarly expertise' (Arreola et al., 2003: 1). Arreola (2007) has taken this model and developed a comprehensive evaluation system in which student feedback on instruction is one of numerous approaches to collecting data. Student ratings are useful under the right conditions which, according to Aleamoni (1978, as cited in Arreola, 2007), is when they are used as part of a personal consultation between the instructor and a faculty development resource person.

The model is a multi-dimensional one, beginning with base professional skills that newly hired academic staff have. These include content expertise, techniques for keeping current in the field, practice and/or clinical skills appropriate to the field, and research skills and techniques appropriate to the field. However, these skills are insufficient when discussing instructional duties and other activities academic staff typically perform (institutional service, including potential administrative duties, and research aligned to institutional expectations). Arreola's (2007) approach toward evaluating performance that includes all of these additional layers of expertise has eight steps:

1. Determine the faculty role model.
2. Determine the faculty role model parameter values – codify the priorities and values relative to the role faculty play.
3. Define the roles in the faculty role model – clearly define each role in terms of specific activities that allow for performance measurement.
4. Determine role component weights.
5. Determine appropriate sources of information.
6. Determine information source weights.
7. Determine how information should be gathered.
8. Complete the system – select/design/build the various tools necessary to gather the information needed to conduct the evaluation.

SERVQUAL

For the purposes of this chapter, SERVQUAL represents a line of thinking in which student feedback is primarily for the purpose of determining the quality of educational programmes from a student or other external stakeholder perspective. SERVQUAL looks at ten variables to assess service quality fit: tangibles, reliability, responsiveness, communication, credibility, security, competence, courtesy, understanding/knowing the customer and access.

SERVQUAL is not without its detractors due to applicability to different service industries because of a lack of completeness in measuring certain aspects of service quality (Chiu and Lin, 2004; Sureshchandar et al., 2001). Others have methodological (Smith, 1995) and empirical concerns (Van Dyke et al., 1997). Thus, Carr (2007) proposes SERVPERF (service through the lens of organizational fairness) as an alternative. However, Bayraktaroglu and Atrek (2010) find that SERVQUAL as well as another similar model, SERVPERF (service performance), can be used in measuring service quality in higher education services. And in their use of SERVQUAL, Emanuel and Adams (2006) found that the dimensions of reliability (the instructor's ability to instruct the course dependably and accurately) and responsiveness are the most important dimensions of instructor service to students.

Using SERVQUAL assumes that universities are a service industry. For example, Schneider et al. (1994) conceptualised teaching as a service 'in that (a) teaching processes and experiences are relatively intangible; (b) teaching is typically produced, delivered, and consumed simultaneously; and (c) teaching typically requires the presence of customers' (p. 685). 'SERVQUAL assumes that the difference between the customer's expectations about a service and his or her perceptions of the service actually determines quality' (Bayraktaroglu and Atrek, 2010: 47). According to Parasumaran et al. (1985), it is more difficult to understand and evaluate the impact of services because they are intangible, heterogeneous and inseparable. The model distinguishes between service quality and satisfaction. '[P]erceived service quality is a global judgment, or attitude, relating to the superiority of the service, whereas satisfaction is related to a specific transaction' (Parasumaran et al., 1985: 16). What is at play is a 'disconfirmation paradigm' that suggests that, prior to an interaction, consumers form expectations about ensuing product/service experiences (Prugsamatz et al. 2007). Figure 2.1 below illustrates how the customer service model focuses on sources of complaints and how failure can be traced back to reduce similar negative incidents in the future.

Figure 2.1 **Root causes of customer failures**

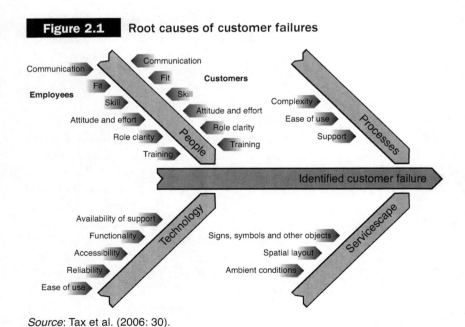

Source: Tax et al. (2006: 30).

Discussion

In 1974, Hartnett and Centra found that there tends to be a good deal of consensus between administrators, faculty (academic staff) and students about the academic environment found at a university. The principal exception found was in how students differed in their views about democratic governance, with lesser variation found regarding the institution's concern for innovation and the overall extent of staff morale.

Glasser (1998), in his analysis of quality in education for education in the twenty-first century, argues that students are asked to perform tasks in order to be evaluated, creating reviewable work that, in turn, allows them to recognise quality in the classroom. ENQA (2005) guidelines for HEI quality assurance systems include, among other items, student satisfaction with programmes and teacher effectiveness.

The challenge is to ensure these are mutually compatible in terms of improving student learning while enhancing professional development opportunities rather than punitive personnel decision making. Aleamoni (1999) warned of the potential misuse of student ratings due to misinterpretation and misuse by administrators for punitive personnel decisions. This warning could be extended to the use of data for quality assurance purposes as well. Embedded within this challenge is the balance between academic freedom in contrast to the need for conformance. Burgan (2006) suggested that variety of instruction is informative to students and universities. Conversely, UNESCO defined student evaluation of teachers as the determination of the need for conformance 'between student expectations and the actual teaching approaches of teachers' (Vlăsceanu et al., 2007: 93) Programmes such as the Tuning Project being performed in Europe and Latin America – whose purpose it is to establish a methodology for designing/redesigning, developing, implementing and evaluating different study programmes (González and Wagenaar, 2008) – are concerned with conformity leading to disengagement of academic staff. This is because their interests (and those of the disciplines they represent) would become marginalised when compared to policy steering and satisfaction interests.

'New research shows that outstanding performance is the product of years of deliberate practice and coaching; not of any innate talent or skill' (Ericsson et al., 2007: 115). Contrary to a potential reading of comments in this chapter, the models being put forward at the international level regarding the evaluation of instruction understand this and insist that adequate support for improving instruction from the professional development and enhancement of student learning perspective be provided. What the role of student feedback brings to the debate of institutional quality is where the emphasis lies; particularly in regard to institutional autonomy when it comes to disciplinary interests, freedom of expression or inquiry, and pedagogical matters. Another way of looking at this is the potential that the sharing of conclusions happens because there is a preference to convene around failures rather than successes (cf. Darling et al., 2005).

This chapter is written primarily from an 'American' perspective. Observations are based on how this perspective fares in relation to international practice. The author first became aware of the development of a continuum in the practice of evaluating instructors when listening and reading approaches taken by academic staff in Europe to establish their own student evaluation forms. Some of these individuals used the SERVQUAL model because of a lack of awareness of long-standing models and methods for evaluating instruction and student ratings.

Writers such as Wiers-Jennsen et al. (2002) document how academic staff and institutions in Europe have been looking for workable models of instruction evaluation. The continuum represents the divergence that exists based on demands placed on the institution and staff. Student feedback is not the problem. What is pressing is the role student feedback plays in the form of student ratings and evaluation of faculty and how the data are going to be used. There are other issues that are not discussed here because they are important topics in their own right (e.g. electronic forms and the ability for students to see the impact of their feedback). What is the priority for academic staff? Is it an education that leads to jobs or developing critical thinking skills and aesthetic and ethical abilities that lead to needed social skills (e.g. Institutional Management in Higher Education, 2007) or is it research? Arreola and his colleagues have developed a conceptual model and a process for the instruction of evaluation that reflects the nuance of academic work. Is a customer service model sufficiently sophisticated and does it adequately align student feedback to ensure that all aspects of academic work are properly documented and enacted upon in a manner beneficial to academic staff, students, HEIs and nations? These are the questions which still remain to be answered.

References

Aleamoni, L.M. (1978). 'The usefulness of student evaluations in improving college teaching'. *Instructional Science*, 7, 95–105.

Aleamoni, L.M. (1999). 'Student rating myths versus research facts from 1924 to 1998'. *Journal of Personnel Evaluation in Education*, 13(2), 153–166.

American Council on Education, American Association of University Professors, and United Educators Insurance Risk Retention Group (2000). *Good practice in tenure evaluation: Advice for tenured faculty, department chairs, and academic administrators*. Washington, DC: American Council on Education.

Arreola, R.A. (2007). *Developing a comprehensive faculty evaluation system: A guide to designing, building, and operating large-scale faculty evaluation systems*. (3rd ed.). San Francisco: Anker Publishing.

Arreola, R, Theall, M. and Aleamoni, L.M. (2003). *Beyond scholarship: Recognizing the multiple roles of the professoriate*. Paper presented at the 2003 AERA Convention, April 21–25, Chicago, IL.

Baldrige National Quality Program at the National Institute of Standards and Technology (2009). *2009–2010 Education Criteria for Performance Excellence*. Gaithersburg, MD: Author. Available online at: *http://www.baldrige.nist.gov/ PDF_files/2009_2010_Education_Criteria.pdf* (accessed 5 January 2010).

Bayraktaroglu, G. and Atrek, B. (2010). 'Testing the superiority and dimensionality of SERVQUAL vs. SERVPERF in higher education'. *Quality Management Journal*, 17(1), 47–59.

Birnbaum, R. (1988). *How colleges work: The cybernetics of academic organization and leadership*. San Francisco: Jossey-Bass.

Boyer, E.L. (1990). *Scholarship reconsidered: Priorities of the professoriate*. Princeton, NJ: Carnegie Foundation for the Advancement of Teaching.

Braskamp, L.A. and Ory, J.C. (1994). *Assessing faculty work: Enhancing individual and institutional performance*. San Francisco: Jossey-Bass.

Brocato, R. and Potocki, K. (1996). 'We care about students . . . one student at a time'. *Journal for Quality and Participation*, 19(1), 74–80.

Burgan, M. (2006). *What ever happened to the faculty? Drift and decision in higher education*. Baltimore, MD: Johns Hopkins University Press.

Carr, C.L. (2007). 'The FAIRSERV Model: consumer reactions to services based on a multidimensional evaluation of service fairness'. *Decision Sciences*, 38(1), 107–130.

Chiu, H-C. and Lin, N-P. (2004). 'A service quality measurement derived from the theory of needs'. *The Service Industries Journal*, 24(1), 187–204.

Cronbach, L.J. (2000). 'Course improvement through evaluation'. In D.L. Stufflebeam, G.F. Madaus and T. Kellaghan (eds), *Evaluation models. Viewpoints on educational and human services evaluation* (2nd ed.), pp. 235–247. Dordrecht: Kluwer Academic.

Darling, M., Parry, C. and Moore, J. (2005). 'Learning in the thick of it'. *Harvard Business Review*, 83(7), 84–92.

Emanuel, R. and Adams, J.N. (2006). 'Assessing college student perceptions of instructor customer service via the Quality of Instructor Service to Students (QISS) Questionnaire'. *Assessment and Evaluation in Higher Education*, 31(5), 535–549.

Ericsson, K.A., Prietula, M.J. and Cokely, E.T. (2007). 'The making of an expert'. *Harvard Business Review*, 85(7/8), 114–121.

European Association for Quality Assurance in Higher Education (ENQA) (2005). *Standards and guidelines for quality assurance in the European Higher*

Education Area. Helsinki: ENQA. Available online at: *http://www.bologna-bergen2005.no/Docs/00-Main_doc/050221_ENQA_report.pdf* (accessed 28 February 2010).

Ewell, P.T. (2002). 'An emerging scholarship: a brief history of assessment'. In T.W Banta and Associates (eds), *Building a scholarship of assessment*, pp. 3–25. San Francisco: Jossey-Bass.

Glasser, W. (1998). *The quality school: Managing students without coercion.* (Revised ed.). New York: HarperPerennial.

Glassick, C.E., Huber, M.T. and Maeroff, G.I. (1997). *Scholarship assessed: Evaluation in the professoriate.* San Francisco: Jossey-Bass.

González, J. and Wagenaar, R. (2008). *Universities' contributions to the Bologna Process: An introduction.* (2nd ed.). Bilbao: Universidad de Deusto. Available online at: *http://tuning.unideusto.org/tuningeu/* (accessed 16 July 2009).

Guthrie, E.R. (1949). 'The evaluation of teaching'. *Educational Record*, 30, 109–115.

Hartnett, R.T. and Centra, J.A. (1974). 'Faculty views of the academic environment: Situational vs. institutional perspectives'. *Sociology of Education*, 47(1), 159–169.

Institutional Management in Higher Education (2007). *Learning our lesson: Review of quality teaching in higher education.* Paris: OECD.

Kitagawa, F. (2003). 'New mechanisms of incentives and accountability for higher education institutions: Linking the regional, national, and global dimensions'. *Higher Education Management and Policy*, 15(2), 99–116.

Kuh, G.D. (2001). 'Assessing what really matters to student learning: inside the National Survey of Student Engagement'. *Change*, 33(3), 10–17, 66.

Lehtinen, U. and Lehtinen, J. (1991). 'Two approaches to service quality dimensions'. *Service Industries Journal*, 11, 287–303.

Marsh, H.W. (1987). 'Students' evaluations of university teaching: research findings, methodological issues, and directions for future research'. *International Journal of Educational Research*, 11, 253–387

New England Association of Colleges and Universities, Commission on Institutions of Higher Education (2006). *Standards for accreditation.* Bedford, MA: Author. Available online at: *http://cihe.neasc.org/downloads/Standards/Standards_for_Accreditation__2006.pdf* (accessed 29 January 2010).

Padró, F.F. (2010). 'University centers of teaching and learning: a new imperative'. *Quality and Participation in Higher Education Supplement of the Journal of Quality and Participation*, 1(1), 3–10.

Pallett, W. (2006). 'Uses and abuses of student ratings'. In P. Seldin and Associates, *Evaluating faculty performance: A practical guide to assessing teaching, research, and service*, pp. 50–65. Bolton, MA: Anker Publishing.

Parasumaran, A., Zeithaml, V.A. and Berry, L.L. (1985). 'A conceptual model of service quality and its implications for future research'. *Journal of Marketing*, 49(3), 41–50.

Parasumaran, A., Zeithaml, V.A. and Berry, L.L. (1988). 'SERVQUAL: a multiple-item scale for measuring consumer perceptions of service quality'. *Journal of Retailing*, 64(1), 12–40.

Pate, W.S. (1993). 'Consumer satisfaction, determinants, and post-purchase actions in higher education'. *College and University Journal*, 68, 100–107.

Pereda, M., Airey, D. and Bennett, M. (2007). 'Service quality in higher education: the experience of overseas students'. *Journal of Hospitality, Leisure, Sport and Tourism Education*, 6(2), 55–67.

Prugsamatz, S., Heaney, J.-G. and Alpert, F. (2007). 'Measuring and investigating pretrial multi-expectations of service quality within the higher education context'. *Journal of Marketing for Higher Education*, 17(1), 17–47.

Ramsden, P. (1991). 'A performance indicator of teaching quality in higher education: The Course Experience Questionnaire'. *Studies in Higher Education*, 16(2), 129–150.

Schneider, B., Hanges, P.J., Goldstein, H.W., and Braverman, E.P. (1994). 'Do customer service perceptions generalize? The case of student and chair ratings for faculty effectiveness'. *Journal of Applied Psychology*, 79(5), 685–690.

Slaughter, S. and Leslie, L.L. (1997). *Academic capitalism: Politics, policies, and the entrepreneurial university*. Baltimore, MD: Johns Hopkins University Press.

Smith, A.M. (1995). 'Measuring service quality: is SERVQUAL now redundant?' *Journal of Marketing Management*, 11, 257–276

St. John, E.P., Kline, K.A. and Asker, E.H. (2001). 'The call for public accountability: rethinking the linkages to student outcomes'. In D.E. Heller (ed.), *States and Public Higher Education Policy: Affordability, Access, and Accountability*, pp. 219–242. Baltimore, MD: Johns Hopkins University Press.

Straker, D. (April 2001). 'What is quality? Part 1.' *Qualityworld*. Available online at: *http://syque.com/quality_tools/articles/what_is_quality/what_is_quality_1.htm* (accessed 15 February 2010).

Stufflebeam, D., Madaus, G. and Kellaghan, T. (eds) (2000). *Evaluation Models. Viewpoints on Educational and Human Services Evaluation* (2nd ed.), pp. 236–247. Dordrecht: Kluwer Academic.

Sureshchandar, G.S., Rajendran, C. and Kamalabanhan, T.J. (2001). 'Customer perceptions of service quality: a critique'. *Total Quality Management*, 12(1), 111–124.

Tax, S.S., Colgate, M. and Bowen, D.E. (2006). 'How to prevent your customer from failing'. *Sloan Management Review*, 47(3), 30–38.

Van Dyke, T.P., Kappelman, L.A. and Prybutok, V.R. (1997). 'Measuring information systems service quality: concerns on the use of the SERVQUAL questionnaire'. *MIS Quarterly*, 21(2), 195–208.

Vlăsceanu, L., Grünberg, L. and Pârlea, D. (2007). *Quality assurance and accreditation: A glossary of basic terms and definitions*. Bucharest: UNESCO.

Weick, K.E. (1995). *Sensemaking in organizations*. Thousand Oaks, CA: Sage.

Wiers-Jennsen, J., Stensaker, B. and Grøgaard, J.B. (2002). 'Student satisfaction: toward an empirical deconstruction of the concept'. *Quality in Higher Education*, 8(2), 183–195.

Student feedback in higher education: a Malaysian perspective

Marlia Puteh and Hadina Habil

Abstract: This chapter analyses how student feedback was used as one of the programme evaluation methods in Malaysia and the extent to which Malaysian universities have reacted to the call to enhance the quality of their academic programmes. The Malaysian Ministry of Higher Education is currently putting demands on the universities to perform competently in their core business of teaching and learning. Undeniably, universities are committed to improving the educational experience they provide, and thus student evaluations of their course experience are a critical component in attaining the information to guide improvement. The chapter poses the following questions: What progress has been recorded and what limitations have been experienced with regard to the implementation of student evaluations in Malaysian universities? Has there been any resistance from faculty members? Can the Malaysian tertiary sector deliver the institutional quality improvement expected by the stakeholders?

Key words: quality assurance; higher education; teaching effectiveness; online evaluation; generic skills.

Abbreviations:

NHEAP	National Higher Education Action Plan
e-PPP	Online Student Evaluation of Teaching System
CTL	Centre for Teaching and Learning
UTM	Universiti Teknologi Malaysia
UPM	Universiti Putra Malaysia
USM	University Sains Malaysia
UCE	University of Central England
SaLT	students as learners and teachers

Introduction

Rapid democratisation of Malaysian education has called for the establishment of a more standardised and organised approach towards quality assurance in the universities. Hence, organisations responsible for quality assurance in higher education institutions in Malaysia are accountable to the general public, and thus need to convince them of the standard of higher education. There are a number of approaches that higher education institutions take to address this issue, for example through collecting student feedback on satisfaction with teaching in their courses. Student feedback is widely used for the purpose of quality assurance of academic programmes especially in the UK, USA and Australia (Coffey and Gibbs, 2001; Richardson, 2005).

Assuring quality is required of a great majority of tertiary institutions around the world. There are additional pressures put on institutions which require accreditation or certification of their programmes from professional bodies. This accreditation or certification requires documentation of quality assurance process within the institutions. The quality assurance practice involves all the stakeholders of the education system – teachers, students, supporting staff, external parties and others. Thus, student feedback is a very important element in programme evaluation for improvement.

Student feedback has been used in many universities around the world to improve their academic programmes. This feedback reflects student experience of the educational provision in their respective tertiary institution, such as their perceptions of teaching and learning, learning support facilities and learning environment. Harvey (2001) reported that student feedback in many institutions provides two functions: internal information to guide improvement, and external information for potential students and other stakeholders. For example, on its website, the University of Malta clearly outlines the 'student feedback cycle' utilised by the University in evaluating its service provision. The feedback is obtained online twice a year, at the end of each semester, and is obtained only from selected units of study. In comparison, the University of Central England (UCE) had a more transparent approach to providing information on student feedback, by making it available on the university website and also publishing the feedback in a printed format (Harvey, 2001). Williams (2002) referred to the act of publishing feedback as the institutional aspiration towards continuous quality improvement. He further argued the advantages of this openness and transparency to the students, employers and the wider community as well as the national funding agencies. This then reflects the quality assurance process implemented by the institution. Other institutions that have used the UCE's model of utilising student feedback include a number of institutions in the UK, such as Sheffield Hallam University, Glamorgan University, Cardiff Institute of Higher Education, Buckingham College of Higher Education and the University of Greenwich. The model was also adopted by other institutions outside the UK, such as Auckland University of Technology (New Zealand), Lund University (Sweden), City University of Hong Kong, and Jagiellonian University (Poland) (Harvey, 2001).

There have been other approaches to collecting student feedback, for example one implemented by Bryn Mawr College in Pennsylvania, USA, through designing a rather radical project called SaLT (students as learners and teachers). The essential part of the project was when students were given the role of consultants. These 'consultants' visited faculty members' classes and shared their perspectives on classroom teaching. This enabled the teachers to gain feedback on students' views and expectations regarding their teaching approaches and make improvements based on the student-consultant perspectives. SaLT not only assisted the teachers in reflecting on their teaching, but students also gained respect from their lecturers for being able to offer insights and suggestions from the end-user perspective.

Malaysia's educational competitiveness ranking

The 2008–2009 Global Competitiveness Report provides a weighted average of many different components referred to as *12 pillars of economic competitiveness*.[1] All 12 pillars matter to a certain extent for all countries; the importance of each one depends on a country's stage of development. The pillars are organised into three sub-indexes, each critical to a particular stage of development: factor-driven economies (stage 1), efficiency-driven economies (stage 2) and innovation-driven economies (stage 3). Higher education is a pillar regarded as one of the key efficiency enhancers for efficiency-driven economies, in which Malaysia positions itself (Porter and Schwab, 2008).

The quality of higher education is crucial for economies that intend to increase the 'value chain', particularly in nurturing the 'knowledge workers'. The World Economic Forum ranks a country's higher education attainment through measuring the increased number of well-educated workers by assessing the secondary and tertiary enrolment rates as well as the quality of a country's education. Table 3.1 demonstrates Malaysia's higher education performance index by analysing those educational factors in 2008.

Finland emerged as the global leader in the higher education and training as it scored exceptionally high in all components, i.e. secondary enrolment (ninth), tertiary enrolment (second) and quality of educational system (first). This is followed by Denmark, which ranked second in its higher education index. However, as Table 3.1 demonstrates, ranks obtained in the higher education and training index do not indicate a country's good quality of educational system as the scores are dependent on three components: secondary and tertiary education enrolment

Table 3.1 Malaysia's higher education performance relative to other selected countries in 2008

COUNTRIES	PILLAR							
	HIGHER EDUCATION & TRAINING		SECONDARY ENROLMENT		TERTIARY ENROLMENT		QUALITY OF EDUCATIONAL SYSTEM	
	Rank	Score	Rank	Hard data[1]	Rank	Hard data[1]	Rank	Score (scale 1–7)[2]
Finland	1	6.07	9	111.6	2	93.2	1	6.2
Denmark	2	5.98	3	119.5	7	79.9	6	5.8
United States	5	5.67	48	93.9	6	81.8	19	5.0
Switzerland	7	5.60	52	92.7	45	45.8	3	6.0
Singapore	8	5.56	21	101.7	31	55.9	2	6.2
Australia	14	5.44	1	150.3	15	72.7	9	5.5
United Kingdom	18	5.27	34	97.9	26	59.3	28	4.6
Malaysia	35	4.63	95	69.1	71	28.6	18	5.0
Italy	44	4.43	26	100.3	19	67.0	84	3.2
Thailand	51	4.31	85	78.1	44	45.9	46	4.0
Indonesia	71	3.88	102	64.2	91	17	39	4.2
Paraguay	117	2.85	98	66.5	75	25.5	134	2.0

[1] Gross enrolment rate
[2] The scales apply the following range:
1 = does not meet the needs of a competitive economy; 7 = meets the needs of a competitive economy

Source: Porter and Schwab (2008: 16–17, 412–14).

rates and the quality of the educational system. The United States, for example, ranked fifth in its higher education and training pillar but achieved poorly (19th) in the quality of its educational system. In some of the component indexes, Malaysia was very close to some of the more advanced economies – for example, the quality of educational system index placed Malaysia 18th, next to the United States (19th) and the United Kingdom (28th).

On balance, Table 3.1 shows the outstanding quality of the Malaysian educational system. What have been the factors enabling this achievement? The Malaysian National Higher Education Action Plan (NHEAP) 2007–2010 has outlined seven strategic aims for the transformation of higher education in Malaysia. These include:

1. Widening access and enhancing equity;

2. Improving the quality of teaching and learning;

3. Enhancing research and innovation;

4. Strengthening institutions of higher education;

5. Intensifying internationalization;

6. Enculturation of lifelong learning;

7. Reinforcing the Higher Education Ministry's delivery system.

However, this chapter will only explore strategic aim number 2 in attempting to discuss the issue of student feedback. The aim focuses attention on evaluation as an 'important aspect of pedagogy' (Ministry of Higher Education Malaysia, 2007) and judges good teaching through good evaluation from the students. This chapter will also investigate the reaction of Malaysian universities and the extent to which they responded to the Ministry's call towards improving their institutional quality in teaching and learning.

Student feedback in higher education

Student feedback is defined as 'the expressed opinions of students about the service they received' (Harvey, 2001). According to Cohen (1980), student-rating through student feedback served three purposes: informing the administrators of teaching effectiveness, providing feedback to instructors on their teaching and helping students to choose good-quality courses and excellent instructors. Cohen also claimed that students' rating can enhance teaching as it can encourage a person's teaching abilities and motivate instructional effectiveness of a course over a semester. Cohen believed that student-rating assists in the administrators' decisions with regard to salary increase, promotion and tenure of individual instructors. The importance of students' rating on administrative decisions is further acknowledged by Beran, Violato and Kline (2007). However, Beran et al. argued that students' rating gives more benefit to administrators rather than instructors because it enables administrators to monitor specific course improvements, such as changes in teaching skills, and distinguish the teaching quality among the range of academic programmes offered in the department.

On the contrary, Harvey (2001) argued that there are two key motives in gathering students' feedback: obtaining internal information for institutional quality improvement and gathering external information for potential students and other stakeholders. However, Harvey observed that views gathered from students are less likely to be transformed into reports or information communicated within the institution to affect change in the institution. Furthermore, very few institutions make the results of students' feedback available to the public, and such feedback has always been regarded as confidential to the institution. Is this true in the context of Malaysian universities? What kinds of limitations have been experienced with regard to the implementation of student evaluations in Malaysian universities? The following sections will investigate these issues in greater detail.

Student feedback in Malaysian universities

Earlier sections in this chapter have positioned Malaysian higher education in the context of global achievement with regards to the quality of the educational system. Malaysian universities are moving toward improving the quality of programmes offered, as is exemplified by several universities discussed in this section. However, the extent of this development is worth addressing, considering the lack of previous research on students' rating in Malaysia. The requirements of the NHEAP have pressured Malaysian universities to engage with some kind of evaluation of classroom teaching by students. As a result, the quality of teaching and learning showed tremendous improvement in 2008, with Malaysia ranking in 18th position in the quality of its educational system compared to selected countries (see Table 3.1 above).

Malaysian universities, exemplified by Universiti Putra Malaysia (UPM), have responded to the demand to improve the quality of its teaching and learning agenda by introducing student course evaluations. These official student evaluations are carried out every semester and conducted by administrative support staff. Instructors are not involved in the process of gathering this information. All teaching staff (including part-time) are evaluated by a certain percentage of their students and these scores are used in the performance appraisal of the staff. The responsible unit then accumulates all the scores and examines the achievement at the university level. Lecturers with scores less than the standard required by the university are required to attend teacher training courses, counselling sessions and similar activities. Although UPM does not have an advanced system of aggregating and reporting the results, the feedback is doing much to improve the teaching and learning at the university.

Similarly, University Sains Malaysia (USM) is utilising a system of student feedback to review faculty's teaching effectiveness in terms of course delivery, content and assessment. Lecturers teaching the different courses are required to distribute the evaluation forms to their students during the last few weeks of the semester. A student representative later sends the completed evaluation forms to the Academic Office. Lecturers are informed of the result of the evaluation once the score becomes available. A low score by students pertaining to an individual lecturer's teaching performance in all the three aspects outlined above indicates problems that need to be addressed. Thus, student feedback which is conducted at the end of every semester assists quality assurance practice by providing a 'check and balance' system of teaching. It also serves as an initial warning so that remedial action can be conducted before any bigger problem emerges. For example, individual lecturers with low scores will be called by their supervisors to probe for any problems that might contribute to the poor score.

In the case of another Malaysian university, student feedback is carried out in the form of learning activities rather than the traditional end-of-semester course evaluation. Leong et al. (2007) supported utilising student feedback in the form of learning activities which, they argued, the students preferred. Their study discovered that students in two Malaysian medical schools used a variety of other learning resources apart from using textbooks as a primary source of information. Their study revealed a very important fact about how students view the teaching approaches adopted by their lecturers. Despite the attempts by lecturers to incorporate self-directed learning through problem-based learning (as stated in the curriculum goals), students were more interested in the content of the lecture than the process of learning. The implication of this finding is that lecturers should incorporate a variety of learning resources when preparing for lectures. The findings of the study have highlighted that, by adapting their teaching methodology based on the feedback from their students, lecturers would be able to meet the expectation of the students. This has proved an effective way of improving the quality of education.

Case study of a Malaysian university

Universiti Teknologi Malaysia (UTM) began in 1906 as a class for technical studies at the Kuala Lumpur City Council Building. Over the last 100 years, the university has continued to grow and change until it finally became what it is today, a university that focuses on producing graduates in the area of science and engineering. The purpose of student evaluation of teaching at UTM is to provide teaching staff with information about their teaching, through which the lecturers can make informed decisions about improving their students' learning outcomes (Universiti Teknologi Malaysia, 2007).

UTM has a standard instrument for gathering data from students about their response to teaching and learning, known as Online Student Evaluation of Teaching System (e-PPP). UTM's Centre for Teaching and Learning (CTL) is given the task of administering the instrument every semester and functions as co-ordinator of the e-PPP. However, CTL's task is merely managing the data. It is not involved in administering the surveys, which in this case is the responsibility of the respective faculties. Once CTL has tabulated the scores, it informs the respective faculties of their performance and reports this to the senior management.

The faculties' performance in the e-PPP is monitored by the Deputy Vice-Chancellor (Academic). However, currently, student feedback from the e-PPP has practically no impact on lecturing, nor does it affect decisions on academic development. Cohen (1980) cited four likely causes for lecturers' failure to benefit from student feedback: feedback does not offer new information to the instructors; it is challenging to transform teaching within a short period of time; normative data is needed to inform the instructors of their strong and weak points; and some instructors may not know how to improve their teaching from students' feedback. Cohen's analysis only addresses individual instructors and is very dependent on the instructors' own attitude to feedback. However, in the case of UTM, the way the e-PPP scores are used to affect institutional change warrants further investigation.

UTM began collecting student feedback in early 2000. Initially, students were required to assess individual lecturers' teaching approach at the end of every semester using printed evaluation forms. In 2003, this evaluation was converted into the electronic format known as the Online Student Evaluation of Teaching System (e-PPP). The survey consists of three parts. The first section requires the students to provide the subject code and the lecturer's name. The second section (22 items) evaluates the lecturer's instructional approaches, namely quality of instruction, teaching delivery, assessment and rapport with the students. Students' responses in this section are rated on a five-point scale from 'very poor' to 'excellent' (with higher values indicating greater effectiveness). The third section (seven items) requires the students to rate the lecturer's integration of generic skills, specifically communication skills, team-working skills, problem-solving skills, adaptive skills, lifelong learning skills andself-confidence as well as moral and ethical competence demonstrated in the classroom. This section requires students to rate the lecturer on a four-point scale from 'none' to 'a great deal'.

In addition, UTM has also introduced annual Teaching Awards which are awarded to two academics (one from an Engineering faculty and one from a non-Engineering faculty) who have demonstrated excellent performance in teaching and learning. Each recipient receives a monetary reward of RM5,000 a certificate, a medal and a grant incentive worth RM2,000 for enhancement and innovation in teaching and learning. In this regard, the e-PPP scores function as the students' 'voice' in determining the award recipients. Potential candidates for this award are required to score above the minimum score[2] of the university in the e-PPP for three consecutive years.

Discussion and lessons learned

A valuable lesson from this e-PPP exercise is the realisation that technology is only a tool in administering the process of evaluation. Online assessment demonstrated by the e-PPP requires students to use a reliable Internet connection. Problems occur when students are unable to access the Internet and the wireless connection on campus has always been an issue. Other setbacks in applying the electronic online evaluation include a lack of Internet infrastructure, a low ratio of students and computers, and inadequate number of Internet-connected computers on campus. Of course, the electronic version of the evaluation should not be the measure of the quality of the actual teaching and learning. In fact, the administrators have to think of ways to encourage students to evaluate their lecturers. Currently, UTM does not have an established approach to achieving a higher student participation rate in the e-PPP, despite extending the evaluation period to a month, providing free Internet access on desktop computers at several computer centres on campus and designing a schedule for specific groups of students to use the computer lab.

Given the existence of a very demanding student feedback system, many academics are reluctant to commit to ensuring their students' participation in the e-PPP conducted at the end of every semester. This is due to the significant level of effort required from faculty members. For instance, individual lecturers have to repeatedly remind their students to access the e-PPP and evaluate their teaching at the cost of their class hours. Some lecturers are even required to take their students to the computer centres and the library at the expense of their time. Often the result may be that students do not complete their evaluations anyway. Irrespective of their efforts, lecturers whose evaluations have low response rates are victimised because of the students' ignorance.

The authors of this chapter propose that there would be value in establishing a unit dedicated to administering student surveys in every faculty. This can eventually become a standard approach to informing university administrators of the effectiveness of the teaching and learning process. This would enable a clear reporting and action mechanism. Beran et al. (2007) justified the importance of student feedback by arguing that it may be the only source of information on faculty teaching, particularly in some research-intensive universities.

Since student feedback is crucial for the development of academic programmes in universities, the authors believe that it is insufficient to ask for student comments only at the end of the course. There may be students who would want to openly criticise their teachers at the end of each teaching session. Teachers should not perceive this negatively as they should be committed to change for the better. Hence, they ought to provide an avenue for the students to engage in constructive criticism of their teaching through various means or techniques, such as the online forum and encouraging comments and suggestions at the end of teaching sessions. The authors further believe that evaluations ought to be regarded as a positive process and should be used for the enhancement of students' learning and staff development. It is hoped that these issues can be resolved as students' evaluation and feedback in Malaysia evolves and matures.

Notes

1. These 12 pillars of competitiveness are institutions, infrastructure, macro-economic stability, health and primary education, higher education and training, goods market efficiency, labour market efficiency, financial market sophistication, technological readiness, market size, business sophistication and innovation.
2. The minimum score of the university is dependent on the average accumulated scores achieved by all fourteen faculties in UTM for each semester. Out of five points, the average scores have been greater than four points in 2007–2009.

References

Beran, T., Violato, C. and Kline, D. (2007). 'What's the "use" of students ratings of instruction for administrators? One university's experience'. *Canadian Journal of Higher Education*, 37(1), 27–43.

Coffey, M. and Gibbs, G. (2001). 'Research note: the evaluation of the Student Evaluation of Educational Quality Questionnaire (SEEQ) in UK higher education'. *Assessment and Evaluation in Higher Education*, 26(1), 89–93.

Cohen, P.A. (1980). 'Effectiveness of student-rating feedback for improving college instruction: a meta-analysis of findings'. *Research in Higher Education*, 13(4), 321–341.

El-Sabban, F. (2001). 'Evaluation of classroom teaching by students and peers for many purposes in academia'. *JUMMEC*, 1, 24–29.

Harvey, L. (2001). *Student Feedback: A Report to the Higher Education Funding Council for England*. Birmingham: Centre for Research into Quality, University of Central England in Birmingham.

Harvey, L. (2003). 'Editorial: student feedback'. *Quality in Higher Education*, 9(1). 3–20.

Leong, K.C., Teng, C.L and Ng, C.J. (2007). 'Learning resources and activities: students feedback from two Malaysian medical schools'. *Medical Journal of Malaysia*, 62 (3), 265–267.

Ministry of Higher Education Malaysia. (2007). *National Higher Education Action Plan 2007–2010*. Putrajaya: Ministry of Higher Education Malaysia.

Porter, M.E. and Schwab, K. (2008). *The Global Competitiveness Report 2008–2009*. Geneva: World Economic Forum.

Quality Assurance Division (2005). *Code of Practice: Quality Assurance in Public Universities of Malaysia*. Putrajaya: Ministry of Higher Education.

Richardson, J.T.E. (2005). 'Instruments for obtaining student feedback: a review of the literature'. *Assessment and Evaluation in Higher Education*, 30(4), 387–415.

Universiti Teknologi Malaysia. (2007). *Policy and Code of Practice for Teaching and Learning.* Skudai: Centre of Teaching and Learning.

University of Malta. Available online at *www.um.edu.mt* (accessed 3 August 2009).

Williams, J. (2002). *The Student Satisfaction Approach: Student Feedback and Its Potential Role in Quality Assessment and Enhancement.* Paper presented at the 24th EAIR Forum, Prague, 8–11 September 2002.

Improving university teaching through student feedback: a critical investigation

Torgny Roxå and Katarina Mårtensson

Abstract: This chapter describes the use of student evaluations in the Swedish context in general, and in one university faculty in particular. The case study illustrates a systematic, well-organised way to collect and collate data from student evaluations on teaching. The study also includes a systematic process to interpret data, where lecturers, students and programme leaders join together. The crucial features of this system are described and analysed. One important conclusion is that, unless the data collected through student evaluations is interpreted and, most importantly, acted upon, the whole process of evaluation runs the risk of becoming a meaningless burden to all involved. Following from this, implications for leadership are also discussed.

Key words: strategic educational development; Swedish tertiary education; student evaluations; leadership; course experience questionnaire.

Abbreviations:

CEQ	Course Experience Questionnaire (a student feedback questionnaire used in the case study)
HSV	Högskoleverket (Swedish National Agency for Higher Education)
KTH	Kungliga Tekniska Högskolan (KTH Royal Institute of Technology)
LTH	Lunds Tekniska Högskola (Lund University Faculty of Engineering)
SOU	Statens Offentliga Utredningar (Swedish Government official report)

Introduction

Sweden has a long tradition of student influence in higher education, dating back to the 1960s. Sweden has since then had powerful student unions as well as student representatives on committees and boards within universities. The practice of student feedback through course[1] evaluations has gradually been established over the last decade. No doubt, this has fulfilled an array of important functions: allowing students to express their opinions about their education, acting as 'fire alarms' when courses have been run badly, providing data sources for course improvements, and also being used as sources for lecturer promotions. This chapter acknowledges all that; however, it moves beyond the importance of collecting feedback and problematises and explores some critical features of student evaluations as a mechanism for guiding development. This will be done in the form of a detailed case study, in which a faculty introduced a large-scale system of collecting student feedback through course evaluations with the purpose of improving teaching and learning. The results are discussed mainly in terms of the importance of student and lecturer engagement, making use of collected data and leadership.

Background

Student evaluations are by no means straightforward to use as tools for development. They need to be interpreted in the light of the context in which they take place and in terms of different possible biases that might occur. Gender might, for instance, play a role, as reported by Centra and Gaubatz (2000) and Sprague and Massoni (2005) – students may favour lecturers of the same gender as themselves. Kwan (1999) and Liaw and Goh (2003) claim that student judgements are affected by class size and study level. It has also been shown that students' perceptions of what constitutes good (or bad) teaching influence the way they evaluate their teaching and learning experience (Prosser and Trigwell, 1999; Ramsden, 2005). This chapter does not elaborate on the issue of student evaluations per se, but rather on the use of student evaluations as a foundation for educational development.

The Swedish Higher Education Act 2000 requires that all students who have completed a course (as part of a programme or as an independent course) should be given the opportunity to express their opinions in a course evaluation organised by the institution.

Higher education institutions shall enable students who are participating in or have completed a course to express their experiences of and views on the course through a course evaluation to be organised by the higher education institution. The higher education institution shall collate the course evaluations and provide information about their results and any actions prompted by the course evaluations. The results shall be made available to the students. (Swedish National Agency for Higher Education, 2000, Chapter 1, Section 14)

The decision to make course evaluations mandatory for institutions came after a long debate in Swedish higher education. The origins of this debate can be traced back to the 1960s. The debate first culminated in the 1980s, when student unions throughout the country demanded course evaluations as a tool for student influence and educational development. This resulted in a national inquiry into higher education, which in 1992 suggested that student participation in processes aimed at establishing and developing quality in university courses should become an organic part of Swedish higher education (SOU,[2] 1992: 1).

As a consequence, evaluations have gradually become a part of the Swedish higher education system, over the following ten years. Today, student evaluations are a widespread phenomenon in the Swedish higher education sector. However, what becomes apparent in the quotation above is that there is no regulation on how the evaluations should be designed, what purpose they should fulfil, nor how they are going to be used; except that the results should be made available to the students. The situation today, therefore, includes a multitude of ways to conduct course evaluations, as well as a multitude of ideas on what questions should be asked of the students, and how the resulting data is to be stored, distributed, analysed or used. In short, the Swedish higher education system is crowded with data generated by students during processes that they, most likely, thought were for the development of university teaching and student learning. But there is no clear picture of how all this data (and effort) is utilised for improvement purposes.

This 'scattered' picture is reinforced by a collection of examples on how student evaluations are carried out in Sweden published by The Swedish National Agency for Higher Education[3] (Heldt-Cassel and Palestro, 2004). This publication incorporates description of approaches to conducting student evaluations in eleven Swedish higher education institutions. In the summary, Heldt-Cassel and Palestro conclude that 'as the contributions in this book illustrate, the views on what a course evaluation should look like or how it should be designed vary' (ibid., p. 9).[4] The picture of course evaluations in Sweden is rather scattered. Different institutions, faculties and departments conduct student evaluations in their own ways. It is, therefore, hard to comment on the effectiveness of these examples. In the introduction, Heldt-Cassel and Palestro state that the purpose of course evaluations is to enhance the quality of higher education through student feedback. However, the contributions in the anthology do not reach the necessary depth where trustworthy claims about such use could be made. They merely describe how evaluations are intended to work, not what actually goes on. In the authors' own institution, a follow-up study on the use of student evaluations (three years after the 2000 Higher Education Act regulation came into effect) showed that student evaluations were introduced in most courses, but the use of the results was patchy as well as the communication to the students about actions taken as a result of the course evaluations (Lund University, 2004). This corresponds to what was reported a decade earlier by the national SOU Report referred to above, in its foreword stating that 'the use of course evaluations is rarely working optimally. Above all, there are shortcomings in terms of communicating the results to students' (SOU, 1992: 7).

In order to expand on this, as a starting point we use two specific Swedish published examples because of their somewhat critical elaboration. These two examples discuss the relationship between evaluations and development.

At the Royal Institute of Technology (KTH), a prestigious Swedish higher education institution, a course analysis consisted of quantitative data: number of students registered; completion rate; students' views on the course; and an analysis made by the lecturer based on the two first sources (Edström, 2008). According to Edström, there was widespread dissatisfaction with this system. The student union complained about the fact that the results had not been further utilised. The National Agency for Higher Education criticised KTH for a lack of consistency in the system and for not informing the students about the results. Many lecturers claimed that the compulsory evaluations were worthless, even 'a venom' (p. 96). Edström's empirical investigation showed that the data collected from students was mainly focused on the students' impressions of the lecturer/s; the lecturers were rated only according to hidden criteria. When the teaching came into view, it only focused on the surface, teaching per se, and revealed almost no relation to student learning. Edström's conclusion was that the student evaluations were 'teaching- and lecturer-focused. As course development is not in the foreground, evaluations merely have a "fire alarm" function' (ibid.: 95). In summary, Edström could see almost no relation between the system for course evaluations and the development of teaching and student learning. The course evaluations were mostly seen as a meaningless burden (ibid.: 96).

The example at KTH is not unique in Swedish higher education. Student evaluations are mandatory: the National Agency for Higher Education conducts audits to ensure their existence and, occasionally, criticises institutions for doing the job poorly, and the students 'guard' them as a *potential* tool for student influence. However, course evaluations too often appear not to 'do the job', namely enabling the development of teaching and student learning.

The second example takes a wider perspective on evaluation as a tool for development of teaching and learning. Its locus is the Faculty of Medicine at Umeå University, another well-established Swedish higher education institution. Fjellström (2008) described how evaluations conducted in the institution led to an extensive dialogue with a number of stakeholders. The process led to an inquiry where those responsible for the medical programme viewed evaluation as 'a resource of interesting and challenging information offering a platform for exchange with engaged stakeholders.' (ibid.: 104). Fjellström made it clear that improvement was at the heart of the process; the results from the evaluation process were both welcomed and used for developmental purposes.

Further, Fjellström (2008) criticised the type of standardised process of evaluation in higher education monitored by the national agency, which threatens to become 'ritualised window-dressing' (similar to students using a surface approach to their studies). Instead, she argued for a more contextualised evaluation where stakeholders formulated their inquiry focusing more on enhancement of learning for medical practice.

It might appear hard to see how Fjellström's vision could be transformed into a large-scale model fitting into modern higher education. Nevertheless, her suggestions might be worth considering, if the alternative is a system which is regarded as a meaningless burden, as in the case of KTH. The critical features of the Umeå example are contextualisation, stakeholder-ownership, dialogue, and inquiry for enlightenment.

In the following section, the authors will investigate the concept of course evaluation in greater depth, through a large-scale and contextualised case study, which is aimed to stimulate a critical conversation about student learning.

Case study: student feedback at the Faculty of Engineering, Lund University

Lund University Faculty of Engineering (LTH) is a research-intensive faculty within one of the oldest higher education institutions in Sweden (Lund University was founded in 1666). LTH has 8,000 undergraduate students (LTH, 2009), 460 doctoral students (of whom most teach 20 per cent of their working time), and 525 lecturers. A majority of the lecturers are also active researchers, where most of this research is funded by external grants won in competition with other researchers. In the overall budget of the faculty, research funding is twice the size of the budget for undergraduate teaching. Almost all of the teaching is organised into five-year programmes, and the students are awarded Master's degrees. The basic organising principle is that programme boards are responsible for the content of, and teaching quality within these programmes. The lecturers, however, are all employed by departments, in turn composed of one or more disciplinary communities. The programme boards, thus, buy courses from the departments and compile these courses into programmes.

LTH has a long tradition of a well-organised and active student union, not only in matters concerning education and its quality. The faculty also prides itself on systematically enhancing student learning. It organises pedagogical courses for lecturers (Roxå, 2005). In Sweden ten weeks of teacher training is mandatory for everyone seeking a tenured academic position in a university (Lindberg-Sand and Sonesson, 2008). The efforts to raise the quality of teaching also include a reward system focused on the Scholarship of Teaching and Learning (Olsson and Roxå, 2008), and since 2003, a bi-annual campus conference on teaching and learning, including peer-reviewed papers (Tempte, 2003). As a complement to these activities the faculty also uses an elaborate system of collecting student feedback on teaching and support of student learning through course evaluations. This system is the focus of the following section, especially its relation to the development of quality in teaching and student learning.

Course evaluations at LTH

The purpose of student feedback on teaching and course evaluations at LTH is explicitly formulated in a policy document:

This policy describing the system of evaluation of undergraduate education at LTH shall contribute to a process where the quality of teaching is consciously and systematically enhanced.[5] (Warfvinge, 2003)

Elsewhere the purpose of evaluations is described thus:

It [the system of course evaluations] is designed to promote an intensified, informed pedagogical discussion among lecturers leading to innovation, improved teaching, and student learning. (Roxå et al., 2007)

To achieve this, student feedback at LTH is collected in two ways.

1. *For operational purposes.* This refers to any feedback a lecturer can organise throughout a course in order to gain a better insight on his or her students' learning so that teaching can be immediately adjusted accordingly. It occurs during the course and is in other contexts often called formative evaluation.

2. *For reporting purposes.* This refers to data collected by the end of the course in order to produce a document describing the quality of the course and is in other contexts often referred to as summative evaluation. The purpose of this document, which is explicitly stated in the policy, is to support the quality enhancing dialogue between the programme boards, the departments, and the students. (Warfvinge, 2003)

The terms *operational* and *reporting* were chosen by this faculty instead of formative and summative to emphasise the *use* of evaluations. *Operational* connotes doing something, while *reporting* is associated with documenting data to be utilised for information purposes.

Operational evaluation is any feedback that a lecturer gains in order to enhance the dialogue with the students, with the purpose of enhancing student learning. More formally, this is often close to Classroom Assessment (Angelo and Cross, 1993). It is frequently directed towards the students' understanding of the material they are supposed to learn or the context (which might support or hinder learning), rather than what the students think about the teaching or the lecturer. Operational evaluations support the lecturer–student dialogue during the course and thereby are very close to what constitutes good teaching. At LTH, it is the responsibility of the lecturers to organise operational evaluations during courses (Warfvinge, 2003), and this may be in whatever format they find suitable. It can be quizzes in the classroom, short diagnostic tests, or meeting with student representatives. The policy does not state how it should be conducted; only that it ought to be conducted, and that the departments have to check that it was carried out.

Reporting evaluation is much more formalised within the faculty. Its purpose is to produce documentation about a course, once it is finished, which allows programme boards, heads of departments, the Dean and other external stakeholders to participate in a conversation aimed at development. LTH utilises the Course Experience Questionnaire, CEQ (Ramsden, 2005) at the end of courses with more than 30 students; and this applies to a majority of courses. The questionnaire clearly supports a focus on student learning. It has 25 items where the students rate to what extent they experienced certain features known to support student learning during the course. The items may, for example, include: 'I got valuable comments from the lecturers during this course'; 'I usually had a clear idea of where I was going and what was expected of me in this course' and similar. There are also opportunities for students to add comments in free text.

The questionnaire focuses on five areas of the teaching process which have been shown to relate to quality in student learning (Ramsden, 2005): *appropriate workload* (do students experience the workload as manageable?); *appropriate assessment* (do students experience the examination as supporting understanding?); *generic skills* (do students experience that the development of generic skills has been supported?); *good teaching* (do students experience support and encouragement from lecturers?); and *clear goals* (do students experience that the lecturers make an effort to help them understand what they are supposed to learn?).

The process of reporting evaluations at LTH runs in six steps:

1. Students fill in the form (paper or web-based) and add comments in free text.

2. The computer system transforms the data into a 'working report' (including all answers from students and the overall results from the examination).

3. The data in the working report is discussed at a mandatory meeting between the responsible lecturer, student representatives and a director of studies responsible for the whole programme of which the course is a part.

4. The lecturer, the students and the director of studies independently write short summaries of or comments on the discussion.

5. Statistically processed data and the comments from the discussion make up the 'final report'.

6. The final report is then published on the faculty intranet and sent via e-mail to all students who took part in the course.

(During 2009 it has been added to the policy that programme boards shall include, in their annual reports, information on data from, and the use of, student evaluations.) The policy document clearly emphasises that this system aims at supporting critical and informed discussions on the development of teaching and learning within the faculty.

By 2009, almost 100,000 questionnaires had been collected and stored in a database accessible to lecturers, students and others within LTH. Course evaluation is discussed in teacher training courses within the faculty. It has also been discussed at the campus conference on teaching and learning (see, for example, Borell et al., 2008; Sparr and Deppert, 2004). The student union is informed repeatedly about the purpose of course evaluations and promotes the system among its many branches.

In summary, LTH has successfully implemented and managed an elaborate system of collecting student feedback on courses. Moreover, the system is aligned with other educational development efforts, such as teacher training courses, a reward system for good teaching, and a bi-annual peer-reviewed campus conference on teaching and learning. LTH also has a faculty leadership devoted to the improvement of teaching and student learning.

Making strategic use of student evaluations

The purpose of course evaluations at LTH is, as stated in the institution's policy, to enhance teaching quality and student learning through the establishment of an intensive and informed discussion within the faculty. Are there signs of this happening?

Students

The students' confidence in the system is supported in an independent external survey (Lund University, 2005). Despite this confidence, it is worth noting that the response rate is diminishing, especially when web-based questionnaires are used. On the other hand, a local investigation (Borell et al., 2008) showed that even if the response rate goes down, the comments given as free texts are longer, from 50 characters (paper) to 100 characters (web). There is no correlation between long and short free-text comments made by students and their overall satisfaction with a course (ibid.). The local data also indicates that lecturers' positive engagement with the course evaluations correlates with the students' response rate (ibid.)

An interesting pattern emerged when the entire material in the database was statistically analysed. It revealed that the CEQ results appear to vary significantly in relation to which programme the students are following. It is possible that students within a programme develop a programme specific study culture, which, in turn, influences their experience of teaching, as measured in student evaluations (Roxå and Modig, 2009).

Lecturers

Since the overall purpose of the evaluation system is to enhance teaching and student learning, it is important to also look at the academic voice. What are lecturer perceptions of the course evaluation system at LTH? In a study conducted by four academics at LTH (Björnsson et al., 2009), the authors claimed that the purpose of the system has not been communicated, or at least not received and integrated by a large section of lecturers within the faculty. This claim was supported by the fact that in 50 per cent of the final reports, the lecturer responsible for a course did not add any comments. Björnsson et al. (2009) also referred to another group of lecturers who criticised the system for not being sensitive to disciplinary differences and for having a hidden agenda of controlling lecturers at the time when the system was implemented (Sparr and Deppert, 2004).

As noted above, lecturers' positive engagement with course evaluations appears to influence the students' response rate, which also relates to the length of comments made by the directors of study. Overall, these patterns indicate that the lecturers' and the directors of study's attitudes towards course evaluations affect students' response rates. LTH lecturers' attitudes towards course evaluations in general – and the CEQ in particular – vary. In a seminar specifically addressing CEQ, 21 out of 28 senior lecturers were positive and seven were negative. Since participation in the seminar was voluntary (and hence only interested lecturers participated), the relation between positive and negative attitudes cannot be generalised to LTH as a whole.

A relatively unexplored area concerns how lecturers react emotionally to receiving student feedback. In Gustafsson (2009), a lecturer describes the frustration experienced when getting negative course evaluation. After a process of carefully examining the data, Gustafsson concluded that, when interpreting course evaluations, other sources, such as exam results, course objectives and similar, also need to be taken into consideration.

Two pilot studies at LTH also explored emotional responses to student feedback. In the first pilot study (Svensson et al., 2009), a small number of lecturers at LTH were interviewed. The results showed that the interviewed lecturers were positive towards student feedback. However, at the same time, the lecturers revealed emotional tension when receiving the feedback provided by the system. Further, there was a small difference between female lecturers, who received more comments on their personal approaches, and their male colleagues, who received more feedback on what they did during their teaching. These results were consistent with previous findings in the literature (Centra and Gaubatz, 2000; Nasser and Fresko, 2002; Santhanam and Hicks, 2002; Sprague and Massoni, 2005). In the second pilot study (Bergström, unpublished), 14 LTH lecturers were interviewed in depth concerning their reactions towards student feedback and the use of such material. Preliminary findings showed that they did not use the statistical material provided to them at all. Instead, all of them described interest in the free-text comments, but most of all, they looked for immediate reactions from the students during class. None of these lecturers described any formalised use of student feedback within their departments or disciplinary communities, even though almost all of them had informal conversations in which these matters were discussed. Another observation from the interviews was the absence of leadership. The lecturers expressed how they individually coped with the results of student evaluations. This lack of a supportive leadership or collegial culture was confirmed in other studies in Swedish higher education (Swedish National Agency for Higher Education, 2008).

In Bergström's (unpublished) study, the individual lecturers appeared sceptical towards formalised student evaluation, such as the CEQ. Partly, this was because it does not take the specific disciplinary conditions into account, and the statistics do not match their experience of the course. They did, however, appreciate the free-text comments. Looking at the operational evaluation, the approach of lecturers was different, as many of them incorporated many of the activities which constitute operational evaluation automatically. To them it constituted good teaching. It is still unclear how the emotional tension experienced by lecturers influences their attitudes towards student evaluations, or their interpretation of the data produced.

The faculty leadership

Currently, there are very few examples of institutional research at LTH where heads of departments or the Dean have used results from student feedback in order to boost a developmental process. There have been no investigations concerning the unofficial use of student feedback; to what extent this type of material is fed into informal backstage conversations about teaching and learning. As for the programme boards this has partly been discussed earlier, with reference to how the programme directors make comments in the final report. The use of data from student evaluations seems to vary tremendously between programmes, as it does between individual lecturers. Some programme boards are active in their use of student feedback in the negotiation about teaching with departments, and with individual lecturers; others show no such activity. Recently, on request by the faculty management, the programme boards have commented, in their annual reports, on the data produced during the reporting evaluation, as well as on measures taken because of this data.

External stakeholders

The National Agency for Higher Education published a quality-review of all civil engineering programmes in Sweden in 2006 and concluded about LTH that: 'CEQ is a good basis for course evaluation, but needs to be developed. Quality assurance is systematic and works well at all levels of the organization' (Swedish National Agency for Higher Education, 2006).

In summary, the authors' observations from LTH show that the institution has developed an elaborate system of student course evaluation. However, the authors also note that the practice of informed discussion of teaching and learning aimed at improvement is developed only in some contexts within LTH.

Discussion

This section highlights some of the challenges faced when utilising the LTH student evaluation system. The LTH student evaluation system is rather well developed. It employs an international, research-based questionnaire, it has built-in components of dialogue between lecturers, students, and directors of study and the results are made publicly available for stakeholder scrutiny. Further, it is supported by other academic development activities, such as mandatory teacher training courses.

Is it only working in theory? The answer, in the light of the observations presented above, is both yes and no. The system generates data and the student feedback is made available. What we have found is a clear variation in the way lecturers and programme boards across LTH utilise this information. Some lecturers and programme boards are actively using the information while others are not.

Previous research has shown that lecturers' use of student feedback varies with their conception of teaching and learning. Hendry et al. (2007) researched a sample of 123 university lecturers, focusing on the relationship between these lecturers' conceptions of teaching and their use of student feedback. Their results showed that lecturers 'strong on conceptual-change, student-focused (CCSF) approach are responsive to feedback and positive about strategies for improving their teaching'. They therefore recommended teacher training courses for all lecturers in order to improve the use of student feedback.

Variation in the use of student feedback at LTH might be explained by the variation in lecturers' conceptions of teaching. However, Hendry et al.'s (2007) recommendation of widespread education of the lecturers does not explain the LTH case, since such a system is already in place and still there is a vast variation in the use of student feedback. An explanation applicable to the LTH case is provided by Roxå and Mårtensson (2009), who have shown how individual lecturers discuss teaching with colleagues, but how these colleagues are carefully chosen and talked to in private in so-called *significant networks*. These networks, it is argued, are the locus of construction and maintenance of lecturers' conception of teaching and learning. This points towards an approach to academic development which moves beyond training of individuals and enters a more 'culture-specific' approach aligned with the research on teaching and learning regimes (Trowler, 2009).

Another approach to enhancing the use of student feedback may be to *require* lecturers to report on how they respond to student feedback. This would place the students' experiences at the centre of the development of teaching and learning. However, two counter-arguments can be used against such a development. Firstly, there is no guarantee that what lecturers would report actually would be the truth. More likely they would, if they have a more transmitting-like conception of teaching, adopt a somewhat surface approach to the student feedback and to the instruction to report on the use of it. Secondly, students' perceptions of teaching during a course vary depending on the approach to learning they use. Students using a deep approach demonstrate 'a more sophisticated understanding of the learning opportunities offered to them than did students with surface approaches' (Campbell et al., 2001). Therefore, teachers using an information transmission approach to teaching would likely interpret positive feedback from surface-approach students as an encouragement rather than a reason for critical reflection.

In addition to these arguments, a further managerial effort to demand the use of student feedback, especially if it is done instrumentally, might possibly threaten the relationship between lecturers and management but, most importantly, also between lecturers and students. In a thoughtful contribution to the discussion, Singh (2002) reflects on student evaluation of teaching in terms of student ratings of teaching. Drawing on Habermas, Singh argues that an unreflective use of student feedback contributes to a perspective where the students become education 'consumers', and the lecturers become education 'providers'. 'So, instead of ticking multiple-choice boxes, our students could attempt to answer some open-ended questions which would encourage them to reflect on their educational experience, and consider their role and responsibility in it' (Singh, 2002: 697). Again, the argument is that what is needed is complex and context-specific material to be utilised for enhancing the dialogue between the key players in education: students and lecturers. It reflects Fjellström's argument (Background section above): 'From being a somewhat threatening instrument of appraisal and grading, the living process of participation, dialogue and deliberation gradually opened up a view where evaluation was regarded as a resource of interesting and challenging information' (Fjellström, 2008).

In summary, the case of LTH mirrors other accounts of the use of student evaluations. The key features of this discussion and lessons learned include the following:

Using the data

One might produce data in higher education mirroring students' experiences of teaching, but the key issue is whether the data is used or not. A well-designed system for course evaluation might look impressive. But if it only fulfils the purpose of collecting feedback, it is merely a waste of lecturers' and students' time. The interpretation of data also needs careful consideration and integration with other sources of information in order to provide the starting point of any development activities, not least because of the possible existence of student study cultures, mentioned above. It is thus possible that the results from student evaluations to some extent are influenced by these cultures. Careful and critical analysis of the data is therefore necessary.

Influencing lecturers

Increasing the *use* of student feedback appears to be more a matter of having an impact on lecturers than designing questionnaires or statistical procedures. Academics are trained in critical thinking; they easily 'tear to pieces' any method for collection of feedback if they do not believe in it, or see the sense in doing it. A logical consequence is that measures that have the potential to influence lecturers' thinking must be included from the beginning in the design of any system of collecting student feedback.

Different ways of influencing university lecturers' thinking about teaching and learning have been explored for many years and examples in the literature are plentiful. Most of them, however, target the lecturer as an individual. The authors would like to add a cultural perspective, looking at the individual in his/her own context. Lecturers relate most of all to their own disciplines (Henkel, 2005). Moreover, they go through a long and intense period of socialisation before they are acknowledged as full members of a disciplinary community. This, most likely, has profound effects on the individual's professional identity, including the ways of thinking. Therefore, staff development should be stretched beyond the individual and into the realm of academic cultures (for an exploration of academic cultures and change, see Trowler, 2009). If a young lecturer enters a disciplinary community where student feedback is considered a resource for improvement, he or she most likely will embrace it too. If the opposite is the case, the academic's attitude will be influenced accordingly. (It should, however, be noted that these processes of influence are not only one-way.)

Leadership

A lot of the changes in Swedish higher education over recent years have put considerable pressure on individual lecturers to develop their courses and their teaching (Swedish National Agency for Higher Education, 2008). Staff development activities have also, to a large extent, focused on supporting the individual lecturer. Course evaluations may add to this focus, laying the full weight of expected improvements on the individual. As the case study presented in this chapter illustrates, there is also a need for leadership in the pursuit of development of teaching and learning at all levels of the institution. The Faculty of Engineering management installed a system partly due to external pressure as a result of the Swedish Higher Education Act of 2000. By doing so, they ran the risk of focusing on quality assurance only, rather than quality enhancement. As it appears to date, the vast amount of collected data has been little used by the faculty leadership. The role of leadership in relation to student feedback on teaching is therefore still unresolved at LTH. Data needs to be utilised by leaders within an institution, and this follow-up must result in action, or leaders must communicate why feedback has not resulted in action. However, the authors would like to warn against the temptation for management to utilise student feedback to put unreasonable pressure on lecturers concerning their performance. This may backfire, since it may 'instrumentalise' the relation between students and lecturers, as expressed by Singh (2002). These authors recommend careful consideration of disciplinary and cultural differences, and also being explicit about the purpose of student feedback and how to utilise the feedback.

In conclusion, the authors fully acknowledge the value of student feedback and course evaluations as one important tool for development of teaching and learning in higher education. However, it is not easily utilised for developmental purposes. The authors have elaborated the complexity and some of the challenges and critical features of such processes, so that student feedback does not become an instrumentalist exercise or, indeed, a waste of time.

Acknowledgement

We are extremely grateful to Mattias Alveteg, LTH, for invaluable critical comments on the content of this chapter.

Notes

1. The Swedish higher education system is to a large extent modularised into courses, which lead to different degrees. Courses can be mandatory or selective within different programmes.
2. Statens Offentliga Utredningar (Swedish Government official report).

3. A national body that oversees quality in Swedish higher education.
4. Translated from Swedish by the authors.
5. Translated from Swedish by the authors.

References

Angelo, T. and Cross, P. (1993). *Classroom Assessment Techniques.* San Francisco: Jossey-Bass.

Bergström, M. (unpublished). *Lärares upplevelser av kursutvärderingar* [Lecturers experiences of course evaluations].

Björnsson, L., Dahlbom, M., Modig, K. and Sjöberg, A. (2009). 'Kursvärderingssystemet vid LTH: uppfylls avsedda syften?' [The course evaluation system at LTH: are the intended purposes achieved?] *Inspirationskursen vid LTH.* Lund: LTH.

Borell, J., Andersson, K., Alveteg, M. and Roxå, T. (2008). 'Vad kan vi lära oss efter fem år med CEQ?' [What can we learn from five years with CEQ?] In L. Tempte (ed.) *Inspirationskonferensen vid LTH,* Lund, LTH.

Campbell, J., Smith, D., Boulton-Lewis, G., Brownlee, J., Burnett, P.C., Carrington, S. and Purdie, N. (2001). 'Students' perceptions of teaching and learning: the influence of students' approaches to learning and teachers' approaches to teaching'. *Teachers and Teaching: Theory and Practice,* 7(2), 173–187.

Centra, J. and Gaubatz, N. (2000). 'Is there gender bias in student evaluations of teaching?'. *Journal of Higher Education,* 71(1), 17–33.

Edström, K. (2008). 'Doing course evaluation as if learning matters most'. *Higher Education Research and Development,* 27(2), 95–106.

Fjellström, M. (2008). 'A learner-focused evaluation strategy. Developing medical education through a deliberative dialogue with stakeholders'. *Evaluation,* 14(1), 91–106.

Gustafsson, S. (2009). *En reflektion kring kursvärderingars roll i högre utbildning.* [A reflection upon the role of course evaluations in higher education]. Written assignment in a teacher training course: 'The good lecture'. Lund University.

Heldt-Cassel, S. and Palestro, J. (2004). *Kursvärdering för studentinflytande och kvalitetsutveckling. En antologi med exempel från elva lärosäten* [Course evaluations for student influence and quality enhancement]. Report 2004: 23R. Stockholm: Swedish National Agency for Higher Education.

Hendry, G., Lyon, P. and Henderson-Smart, C. (2007). 'Teachers' approaches to teaching and responses to student evaluation in a problem-based medical program'. *Assessment and Evaluation in Higher Education,* 32(2), 143–157.

Henkel, M. (2005). 'Academic identity and autonomy in a changing policy environment'. *Higher Education,* 49 (1–2), 155–176.

Kwan, K.-P. (1999). 'How fair are student ratings in assessing the teaching performance of university teachers?'. *Assessment and Evaluation in Higher Education,* 24(2), 181–196.

Liaw, S.-H. and Goh, K.-L. (2003). 'Evidence and control of biases in student evaluations of teaching'. *The International Journal of Educational Management*, 17(1), 37–43.

Lindberg-Sand, Å. and Sonesson, A. (2008). 'Compulsory higher education teacher training in Sweden: development of a national standards framework based on the Scholarship of Teaching and Learning'. *Tertiary Education and Management*, 14(2), 123–139.

Lunds Tekniska Högskola (2009). *Om LTH* [About LTH]. Lund: Lund University, Faculty of Engineering.

Lund University (2004). *Tillämpningen av kursvärdering och studenternas rättighetslista*. [The use of student evaluations and the students' rights list]. Report 2004:228. Lund: Lund University, Evaluation unit.

Lund University. (2005). *Teknologer och civilingenjörer. Erfarenheter av utbildningen vid LTH*. [Technologists and civil engineers. Experiences from education at LTH]. Report 2005: 34. Lund: Lund University, Evaluation unit.

Nasser, F. and Fresko, B. (2002). 'Faculty views of student evaluation of college teaching'. *Assessment and Evaluation in Higher Education*, 27(2), 187–198.

Olsson, T. and Roxå, T. (2008). 'Evaluating rewards for excellent teaching – a cultural approach'. In K. Sutherland (ed.), *Annual International Conference of the Higher Education Research and Development Society of Australasia*, Rotorua, NZ, HERDSA.

Prosser, M. and Trigwell, K. (1999). *Understanding Learning and Teaching. The experience in Higher Education*. Buckingham: Society for Research into Higher Education and Open University Press.

Ramsden, P. (2005). *Learning to Teach in Higher Education*. London: RoutledgeFalmer.

Roxå, T. (2005). 'Pedagogical courses as a way to support communities of practice focusing on teaching and learning'. In S. Barrie (ed.) *Annual International Conference of the Higher Education Research and Development Society of Australasia*, Sydney, Australia: University of Sydney.

Roxå, T., Andersson, R. and Warfvinge, P. (2007). 'Making use of student evaluations of teaching in a "culture of quality"'. Paper presented at *29th Annual EAIR Forum*, Innsbruck, Austria.

Roxå, T. and Mårtensson, K. (2009). 'Significant conversations and significant networks – exploring the backstage of the teaching arena'. *Studies in Higher Education*, 34(5), 547–559.

Roxå, T. and Modig, K. (2009). 'Students' micro cultures determine the quality of teaching!', presentation made at the *17th Improving Student Learning Symposium*, 'Improving Student Learning for the 21st Century Learner', Imperial College, London, UK, 7–9 September, 2009.

Santhanam, E. and Hicks, O. (2002). 'Disciplinary gender and course year influences on student perceptions of teaching: explorations and implications'. *Teaching in Higher Education*, 7(1), 17–31.

Singh, G. (2002). 'Educational consumers or educational partners: a critical theory analysis'. *Critical Perspectives in Accounting*, 13, 681–700.

Sparr, G. and Deppert, K. (2004). 'CEQ som rapporterande utvärdering – en kritisk granskning' [CEQ as reporting evaluation – a critical review]. *Inspirationskonferensen*, Lund: Lund University, Faculty of Engineering.

Sprague, J. and Massoni, K. (2005). 'Student evaluations and gendered expectations: what we can't count can hurt us'. *Sex Roles*, 53(11), 11/12.

Statens Offentliga Utredningar (1992). *Frihet, ansvar och kompetens* [Freedom, responsibility and competence]. Swedish Ministry of Education, Gothenburg: Graphic Systems AB.

Svensson, Å., Fridh, K., Uvo, C. and Hankala-Janiec, T. (2009). *Kursutvärderingar ur ett genusperspektiv*. [Course evaluations from a gender perspective]. Assignment for the course 'Gender-psychological aspects in teaching and learning – women, men and technology', Lund: Lund University, Faculty of Engineering, Genombrottet.

Swedish National Agency for Higher Education (2000). *The Higher Education Ordinance*. Available online at: *http://www.hsv.se/lawsandregulations/thehigh ereducationordinance.4.5161b99123700c42b07ffe3981.html#Chapter1* (accessed 27 July 2010).

Swedish National Agency for Higher Education (2006). *Utvärdering av utbildningar till civilingenjör vid svenska universitet och högskolor*. [Evaluation of Civil Engineering Programmes at Swedish Universities and Institutions of Higher Education]. Report 2006:8R. Stockholm.

Swedish National Agency for Higher Education (2008). *Frihetens pris – ett gränslöst arbete. En tematisk studie av de akademiska lärarnas och institutionsledarnas arbetssituation*. [The prize of freedom – working without limits. A thematic study of the working situation of lecturers and heads of departments]. Report 2008: 22R. Stockholm.

Tempte, L. (2003). *Pedagogisk Inspirationskonferens* Lund: Lund University, Faculty of Engineering, Genombrottet).

Trowler, P. (2009). 'Beyond epistemological essentialism: academic tribes in the 21st century'. In C. Kreber (Ed) *The University and Its Disciplines: Within and Beyond Disciplinary Boundaries*, London: Routledge.

Warfvinge, P. (2003). *Policy för utvärdering av grundutbildning* [Policy on evaluation of undergraduate courses]. Lund: Lund University, Faculty of Engineering.

Student feedback in the Australian national and university context

Denise Chalmers

Abstract: This chapter provides an overview of the practice and use of student feedback in the Australian national and university context. Australia has been a leader in recognising the importance of student feedback in quality assurance at the national level. The national survey of students' experience of their study at university has been a key component in the government's approach to quality assurance in higher education for a number of years and remains a central component of the national quality model.

At the university level, the gathering of student feedback on the quality of teaching and subject is common practice, while gathering student feedback at the programme of study and university level is gaining widespread interest. Increasingly, universities are recognising the value of using subject and programme-level student feedback in their quality performance measures as well as integrating the data from their internal feedback surveys with the national surveys to provide a more detailed and multilayered profile of their students' experiences.

Key words: Australia; national and university context and practices; student feedback on teaching.

Introduction

Higher education institutions have been seeking student feedback on teaching or subjects for several decades. Feedback has been sought more informally in the past, but has become more formalised over time. The information gathered has primarily been used as a teaching evaluation tool to inform teachers and subject co-ordinators for the purpose of ongoing development and improvement of teaching and subjects. In contrast, the development and use of surveys to collect student feedback on their experience of their whole degree or the institution is a more recent development. The systematic use of such surveys to gather data across several institutions or the sector is only now being considered in many countries, with increasing emphasis being placed on student feedback surveys by governments and their agencies as an indicator of teaching quality. In Australia, there have been a number of national initiatives to seek feedback from university students, which have placed Australia as a leader in the sector-wide use of surveys of students' experiences of university teaching.

This chapter provides an overview of the practice and use of student feedback in the Australian higher education context. It does not provide a commentary on the broader issues of using student feedback for quality assurance purposes. For a comprehensive overview of research on student evaluations of university teaching refer to Marsh (2007) and Abrami, d'Apollonia and Rosenfield (2007).

National or sector-wide use of student feedback

The Australian government has taken an active role in promoting quality assurance in universities since the 1980s, when there was a perceived need for universities to improve their efficiency, effectiveness and public accountability. In 1989, the government commissioned a team led by Professor Russell Linke to find performance indicators to assess the quality of higher education. The Linke report asserted that quality would be best assessed using multiple indicators that are 'sensitively attuned to the specific needs and characteristics of particular disciplines, and which adequately reflect the underlying purpose for which the assessment is required' (Linke, 1991: 129). The report also suggested that judgements of the quality of teaching must flow from the analysis of multiple characteristics, and involve a range of procedures including qualitative peer and student evaluation. Three categories of indicators on teaching and learning were identified: quality of teaching; student progress and achievement; and graduate employment.

The subsequent decision by the committee to identify the quality of teaching by students' perceived assessment of teaching quality using the Course Experience Questionnaire (CEQ) was not surprising, given that the developer of the instrument, Paul Ramsden, presented a compelling submission to the committee arguing that 'the CEQ offers a reliable, verifiable and useful means of determining the perceived teaching quality of academic units in systems of higher education that are based on British models' (Ramsden, 1991: 129).

An outcome of Linke's influential report, subsequently supported by the report on benchmarking in Australian universities (McKinnon et al., 2000), was that the CEQ was specifically recommended as an appropriate benchmarking indicator, with the first national administration of the Course Experience Questionnaire (CEQ) to all Australian university graduates in 1993.

Australian Graduate Survey (AGS)

Graduate Careers Australia (GCA) is responsible for the administration of the Australian Graduate Survey (AGS) and works closely with the universities and the Australian government department responsible for higher education to improve the quality of the data, data collection and response rates. The Australian university representative council and GCA jointly released a code of practice and guidelines for the administration of the surveys.

The Survey is comprised of two parts, the Graduate Destination Survey (GDS) and the Course Experience Questionnaire (CEQ) or the Postgraduate Research Experience Questionnaire (PREQ). The AGS is sent to all students who have completed the requirements for a degree in Australian universities, approximately four to five months after graduation. Unlike many surveys of this scale, the AGS is a census survey.

Graduate Destination Survey (GDS)

Australian universities have administered the Graduate Destination Survey (GDS) since 1972. It focuses on details of current employment or study, as well as questions related to job search strategies. Traditionally, this data has been used by universities to advise both prospective and current students and university staff about employment opportunities in different fields of education.

Course Experience Questionnaire (CEQ)

The Course Experience Questionnaire (CEQ) has been administered by Australian universities since 1993. The CEQ was developed as a teaching performance indicator, focusing on aspects of the classroom teaching environment which previous research had found were linked to deep and surface approaches to learning, and higher quality learning (Ramsden, 1991; Wilson, Lizzio and Ramsden, 1997). A subsequent extension of the CEQ was initiated because it was recognised that the original questionnaire emphasised the undergraduate experience taking place within the classroom setting and neglected important dimensions of the current student experience (McInnis et al., 2001).

The CEQ is an extensively validated student feedback survey (Wilson et al., 1997) that has been found to be strongly reliable in a range of different contexts. Few student feedback surveys are as explicitly based on a well-researched theoretical model of learning as the CEQ (Ramsden, 1991). The model recognises that learning is a complex process and the CEQ focuses on student perceptions as a key indicator of this process. However, many of the uses made of the CEQ data ignore this complexity. The CEQ has provided almost two decades of national data that can identify trends for intra- and inter-university comparative purposes that is unrivalled anywhere else in the world.

Traditionally, components of the AGS, and the CEQ scales, have been intended for benchmarking teaching quality, primarily at the degree level, allowing tracking over time of the quality of a specific degree, as well as benchmarking similar programmes of study at different universities. The ability to benchmark has been difficult at times, with relatively low response rates and the use of generic names of programmes of study. Additional criticisms of the CEQ relate to the lagging and aggregated nature of the data, which make it difficult for institutions to use for enhancement purposes and improvement within the university (Barrie and Ginns, 2007). Despite these limitations, many institutions have used the data to inform quality audits, curriculum reviews and internal planning and funding decisions.

Components of the GDS and CEQ have more controversially been used to inform decisions on performance-based funding of institutions, and, more recently, cognate disciplines within institutions through the Learning and Teaching Performance Fund (LTPF). The LTPF scheme was established by the Australian Government in 2003 as part of *Our Universities: Backing Australia's Future*, a scheme to reward the 'higher education providers that best demonstrate excellence in learning and teaching'.

This use of the AGS data has prompted intense discussion within the Australian higher education sector. Some of the concerns have been related to the differential survey practices and response rates between institutions. To address some of these concerns, the government commissioned the Graduate Destination Survey Enhancement Project (GCA, 2009) to improve the quality of responses to the surveys and confidence in their findings and usage (particularly in relation to the LTPF). In a recent evaluation of the LTPF by the responsible government department, it was claimed that the LTPF has been an important catalyst for improvements in data collection for the Graduate Destinations Survey (GDS) and the Course Experience Questionnaire (CEQ) (DEEWR, 2008). For further information on the LTPF and the analysis and use of the AGS data, refer to DEST (2004–2005) and Marks and Coates (2007).

Similar concerns around the lack of consistency in the administration and collection of student data have been experienced in the United Kingdom with the National Student Survey (NSS), first administered in 2005 (Surridge, 2009; Marsh and Cheng, 2008). However, unlike the CEQ, the NSS is administered to students while they are still enrolled in the university, in their final year of study. While, in the UK, funding is not tied to the outcomes of the NSS, they are reported widely in the press and so its impact on university reputation is a concern.

While the LTPF has now been discontinued, the AGS data will continue to be used in university funding decisions. The Australian government has recently released a discussion paper on proposed indicators for higher education performance funding for teaching and learning. Universities will be required to negotiate targets against indicators of performance determined by the government. 'In the simplest terms, if universities achieve their targets, they will receive performance funding' (DEEWR, 2009b: 3). It is proposed that the CEQ continue to be used as the student satisfaction component of the performance target. The administration of the AGS is proposed to be broadened to include all graduates of higher education, not just universities, which is currently the case. In addition, the government is considering developing a new 'University Experience Survey', which would collect information about first-year students' engagement and satisfaction with their university studies (DEEWR, 2009b).

The Postgraduate Research Experience Questionnaire (PREQ)

In response to a growing recognition that the CEQ was not appropriate for the increasing number of postgraduate research students, the Australian government commissioned the development and evaluation of the Postgraduate Research Experience Questionnaire (PREQ). It was anticipated that this would operate in much the same way as the CEQ and provide a multi-dimensional measure of the experience of postgraduate research students as part of a large-scale national benchmarking exercise for Australian universities (Marsh and Cheng, 2008).

The PREQ was first trialled in 1999 to investigate the opinions of recent graduates regarding their higher degree by research experience. It is now administered up to twice a year in association with Graduate Careers Australia (GCA) to students who have completed a doctoral or research masters degree in the previous four or five months. Aggregated reports are periodically generated on the postgraduate research experience (e.g. Edwards et al., 2008).

Serious concerns have been raised about the use of the PREQ for benchmarking the overall postgraduate experience at the broad level of the university, and discipline-within-university groups. Arguments have been presented, based on reviews of research in the areas of students' evaluations of university teaching, teacher/school effectiveness and teacher improvement, that the most important unit of analysis was the individual supervisor (Marsh, Rowe and Martin, 2002). Extensive analysis has subsequently confirmed that PREQ ratings were reliable at the level of individual students but that the results were not particularly relevant for discriminating between universities. The most salient finding was that PREQ ratings did not vary systematically between universities, or between discipline-within-university groups (Marsh, Rowe and Martin, 2002). Marsh and Cheng claim that the results 'call into question research or practice that seeks to use students' evaluations of teaching effectiveness as a basis for comparing universities as part of a quality assurance exercise' (Marsh and Cheng, 2008: 16).

Australasian Survey of Student Engagement (AUSSE)

A survey of student engagement is currently in early development for use across Australian and New Zealand universities by the Australian

Council of Educational Research (ACER, 2009). Based on the USA's National Survey of Student Engagement (NSSE), it is designed to provide data on students' engagement in university study. It is claimed that the principal focus of the AUSSE is to provide within-university information, as it is intended that it will be sensitive to institutional diversity and will have benchmarking potential within Australia and with the relevant data from the United States and Canada.

Student engagement focuses on the interaction between students and the environment in which they learn. Student engagement data provides information on learning processes, and is considered to be one of the more reliable proxy measures of learning outcomes. The data has the potential to assist institutions make decisions about how they might support student learning and development, manage resources, monitor standards and outcomes, and monitor curriculum and services. It can also indicate areas in need of enhancement.

The AUSSE data collection methodology varies significantly from the AGS, for while the AGS has a census methodology, surveying all eligible students, the AUSSE uses a sampling methodology, surveying a representative sample of first- and later-year students at the participating institutions (ACER, 2009). These students are asked to respond to their current experiences, not in hindsight as for the CEQ and PREQ.

In 2007 and 2008, approximately 30 Australian and New Zealand universities participated in the AUSSE to validate the items for use in Australasia. The survey instrument focuses on students' engagement in activities and conditions which empirical research has linked with high-quality learning. Information is also collected online on students' self-reported learning and development outcomes; average overall grades; retention intentions; overall satisfaction; and a range of individual demographics and educational contexts (ACER, 2009). A particular concern to date has been the low response rates, which has impacted on the validation and broad applicability of the survey.

First Year Experience Questionnaire (FYE)

The First Year Experience Questionnaire (FYE) has been administered at five-year intervals since 1994 by the University of Melbourne's Centre for the Study of Higher Education (Krause et al., 2005). Surveying a stratified sample of first-year students of seven universities in 1994 and 1999, and nine universities in 2004, its goal is to 'assemble a unique database on the changing character of first year students' attitudes, expectations, study patterns and overall experience on campus' (Krause et al., 2005: 1). It draws on the CEQ for many of its items. In addition, the 2004 FYE included items and scales focusing on student engagement, and the role of information and communication technologies in student engagement. However, with the response rate for the 2004 survey at only 24 per cent, concerns are expressed about the representativeness of the findings. The government again commissioned the FYE to be administered in 2009, to a sample of first-year students in a limited number of universities.

While the FYE questionnaire is a research instrument rather than a national or sector-wide survey, its impact has been significant as it provided the evidence base for many universities' strategies to improve university transition and first-year retention and progression. As a consequence, a number of Australian universities routinely gather data from their first-year students using a variation of the FYE survey or an adaptation of the CEQ in a university-based survey.

Institutional-level use of student feedback

National initiatives that have influenced collection and reporting of student feedback within universities

The LTPF has been briefly referred to earlier in this chapter in relation to the use of the national student feedback data from the AGS and its impact on data collection processes. However, the LTPF has also had a significant impact on the systematic collection and reporting of student satisfaction within the university, as have the Australian University Quality Agency (AUQA) audits carried out in five-yearly cycles. The impact of each of these on institutional level collection and use of student feedback are briefly described.

Learning and Teaching Performance Fund (LTPF)

In the first three years of this scheme over $220m was allocated to a limited number of universities using quantitative evidence drawn from the indicators identified in the Linke report (1991): quality of teaching (CEQ), student progression and achievement and graduate employment (GDS). While the scheme has been controversial (DEEWR, 2008; Access Economics, 2005), it had a significant impact on university practices in collecting and reporting student feedback within the university.

The LTPF scheme initially involved two stages. Entry into the second stage was contingent upon satisfactorily meeting the requirements of the first. The first stage required institutions to submit evidence of having the following available on their website: a current and recent institutional learning and teaching plan or strategy; systematic support for professional development in learning and teaching for sessional and full-time academic staff; systematic student evaluation of teaching and subjects that inform probation and promotion decisions for academic positions; and evidence that student evaluations of subjects were publicly available. While the second stage attracted the majority of attention, as it determined the allocation of funding, the first stage resulted in many universities revising their policies and systems in relation to the systematic student evaluation of teaching and the reporting of these (DEEWR, 2008).

Australian University Quality Agency (AUQA)

A thematic analysis of the first cycle of AUQA audits of learning and teaching was almost silent on student feedback as a quality mechanism, though some commendations on systems of student feedback for individual universities were highlighted (Ewan, 2009). Despite the limited reference to student feedback in the thematic analysis and the few explicit commendations and recommendations, it would be incorrect to suggest that AUQA did not view student feedback as a critical part of a quality system. AUQA guidelines and training explicitly require that student feedback data is used to inform teaching, curriculum development and university quality processes (AUQA, 2004). The few direct references to student feedback in the university AUQA audit reports are likely because they have well-developed systems of collecting feedback from students. What has been less well developed is the effective and systematic use of the information to inform performance management, curriculum review and enhancement and quality review and monitoring. The AUQA cycle's two quality reviews explicitly link the use of these data to inform quality enhancement and assurance within the university and across universities and disciplines (AUQA, 2008).

Within-university practices and uses of student feedback

Student feedback on teaching

The collection of student feedback on aspects of teaching has gradually evolved over time from a largely informal, formative, private practice, carried out by teachers seeking feedback from their students, to a systematic, whole-of-university approach of gathering feedback from students on the quality of teaching and subjects. The purposes of gathering the feedback from students range from development and enhancement to summative and quality assurance. It is now considered an essential requirement for both quality enhancement and assurance to have a process of systematic gathering of student feedback on teaching.

Historically, student feedback surveys in Australia have been used to provide information to individual teachers for developmental purposes but appraisal and accountability purposes were identified as being legitimate purposes as well (Moses, 1988). The University of Queensland was one of the first Australian universities to establish a whole-of-university approach to seeking feedback from students administered through a central organisation. Prior to this, individuals, schools and departments may have had their own surveys but these were not particularly trusted by staff or students, nor were they systematically administered (Moses, 1988). The institutional teacher evaluation questionnaire had eleven compulsory questions on the lecturer, with the final two global questions asking the student to rate the subject and the overall effectiveness of the teacher. In addition there was the opportunity for the teacher to choose a limited number of additional questions from the item bank. The back of the questionnaire was left largely blank for students' qualitative comments on the staff member's strengths and suggestions for improvements (Moses, 1988). The University of Queensland's student feedback survey questions, structure and process of administration had a significant influence on the subsequent survey design and processes in many Australian universities, as did the University of Sydney's Students' Evaluation of Educational Quality (SEEQ) developed by Marsh (1984). In 1999, a review of institutional student feedback surveys concluded that the majority of Australian student feedback surveys were based on the same two or three original surveys (GCCA, 1999, quoted in Davies et al., 2009). Surprisingly little has changed in this twenty-year period, with current student feedback surveys on teaching retaining a similar structure and focus across most universities. The individual questions themselves show considerable wording variation and are rarely validated using accepted psychometric methods. In the main they have been based on face validity, informed by research on effective teaching and influenced by the institutional culture and values.

There have been two recent reviews of Australian university student feedback surveys (Barrie et al., 2008; Davies et al. 2009). The Davies et al., (2009) study investigates the types of questions used in teacher surveys, while the Barrie et al. (2008) study provides a comprehensive overview of current Australian university Student Evaluation of Teaching (SET) uses and practices at four levels: Teacher, Department, Institution and Sector.

All Australian universities have an established student feedback survey directed at the teacher level with the data used primarily to inform the individual teacher's improvement and development, and as a source of evidence for their performance review and promotion. A number of universities have several types or variations of surveys of teaching to capture the different types of teaching situations, e.g. lecturing, tutorial, laboratory, problem-based, clinical, team teaching or online. The most common survey structure is for a limited number of mandatory questions that are asked across all contexts and include a global question, a limited set of optional questions selected from a database at the discretion of the teacher, and space for students to respond to two or three general questions. However, there is considerable variation across the sector. For example, the University of Western Australia currently offers a fully flexible survey of teaching, with teachers able to select as many questions as they like from a database or to write their own questions. Others offer no flexibility; for example the Universities of South Australia and Southern Queensland student evaluation of teaching survey offer a fixed set of core questions.

Traditionally, student feedback on teaching data has not been routinely incorporated into broader quality reviews of teaching or curriculum. Indeed, many have restrictions on the uses to which teacher-level data could be put, with many universities limiting access to the data solely for the personal use of the teacher. In general, the teacher is responsible for initiating the request for a survey of students on the quality of their teaching and then for using the information for their personal evaluation and improvement.

Student feedback on subjects/units

In response to the need to have access to student feedback data for quality purposes for curriculum development and institutional quality processes and because of the trend for subjects to be taught by teams of teachers, subject-level surveys have been developed. These are generally administered more formally and systematically than teacher-level surveys. For example, many universities specify the frequency and timing of subject surveys: the Universities of Wollongong, Central Queensland and Western Australia survey their students each and every time the subject is offered. The University of Queensland, on the other hand, requires that all subjects are surveyed on a three-yearly cycle, though there is opportunity for them to be surveyed more frequently if necessary.

The questions tend to focus on the subject rather than the teacher, but the structure of the surveys is similar to the teacher surveys. Subject surveys are generally standardised in their wording, number and type of questions, with most allowing no optional questions. Most also provide an opportunity for students to give a response to a limited number of open questions. The subject surveys often sit alongside teacher surveys, and students may be asked to complete both a subject and teacher survey for the one subject. Some universities have combined their teacher and subject questionnaire, for example the Universities of Technology in Queensland and Sydney, but the majority have retained two distinct surveys. As with the surveys on the quality of teaching, subject-level surveys are generally administered towards the end of the study period and so rarely benefit the students who provide the feedback.

The data from the subject surveys is generally made available to a wider audience, including the subject and course co-ordinator, head of school and dean and can be used in curriculum reviews, school reviews and reported to a range of internal and external stakeholders, often in an aggregated report. The extent to which the data from the subject feedback surveys is integrated into a timely cycle of analysis, reporting, action and feedback is highly variable across the Australian universities. The University of Queensland has a comprehensive process where the data is routinely reported to the university, faculty and schools through an online reporting system that brings it together with data on student attrition and progression and the CEQ. However, while other universities are now beginning to move towards using their data in a more integrated way, the extent that the subject data is used in concert with other data such as the CEQ to inform an annual programme of study report or used in conjunction with other student feedback remains more variable.

In the Australian context, all students are provided with the opportunity to give feedback on the teaching and/or the subjects they are studying. Gathering student feedback on the students' broader student experience of the university at the programme of study level or after their first year of study, for example, is more varied.

Student feedback on courses/programmes of study, institutional experience

The majority of Australian universities do not routinely seek students' feedback on their broader experiences of the university or their programme of study, though this has been an area of growing interest in the past decade. With the national administration of the CEQ and First-Year Experience survey, universities have had access to their own data for benchmarking and internal purposes. However, the significant delay in getting access to this national data has resulted in a number of universities instituting a university-level student feedback survey on their broader university experiences.

The University of Sydney was one of the first universities to establish an institutional survey of the broader student experience – the Student Course Experience Survey (Asmar, 2002), which draws heavily on the CEQ and is an integral part of the university quality assurance and enhancement model (Barrie, Ginns and Prosser, 2005). The institutional surveys developed by the University of Queensland and Monash University are more extensive than the University of Sydney survey, seeking feedback from students on their experiences of the programmes they are studying, their experiences of the university facilities and services, as well as the extent to which they feel they are developing the graduate attributes identified by their university. Like the University of Sydney survey, they include some of the major scales of the CEQ such as the *Good Teaching* scale. The University of Queensland also includes some scales from the First Year Experience survey. This allows for benchmarking and comparisons within the institution, across programmes, across other institutions and with the national data sets.

A number of other universities have subsequently introduced a student experience survey. For example, Charles Sturt University administers a modified CEQ survey to students in their first year of study to allow for enhancements to be made to the programmes of study. Curtin University surveys its students on their whole course of study prior to graduation, and has recently introduced a graduate survey to gather recent graduates' perceptions of their course, as well as an employer survey on employers' perceptions of how well they feel the graduates are prepared for employment. The University of South Australia also piloted an employer survey in 2008.

Institutional surveys have been subject to greater scrutiny and validation of the items and scales than the subject and teacher surveys. Reporting of the data is co-ordinated and managed centrally and is broken down by organisational unit and programme of study for comparative purposes. Because of the extensive nature of the student experience surveys and concerns of over-surveying students, they tend to be administered periodically, for example biannually.

Few universities allocate funding based on the outcomes of their student surveys, with the universities of Sydney and Queensland being the first to introduce funding schemes that included student feedback data such as the CEQ and student experience surveys. A number of universities have followed suit, initially in the internal allocation of their LTPF funding, and subsequently to focus the faculty and department attention on the quality of teaching.

Conclusions

This chapter has provided an overview of the practice and use of student feedback in the Australian national and university context. Australia has been a leader in recognising the importance of student feedback in quality assurance at the national level. The introduction of a national survey of students' experience of their study at university has been a key component in the government's approach to quality assurance in higher education for a number of years and it remains a central component of its quality model.

At the university level, the gathering of student feedback on the quality of teaching is ubiquitous; however, its use can predominantly be considered as serving a quality enhancement role to inform personal and career development. The gathering of student feedback on the quality of the subjects is also widespread, with the data informing both quality enhancement and quality assurance purposes at multiple levels within the university. At the programme of study and university level, a growing number of universities are now surveying their students on their teaching and learning experiences as a way to monitor the quality of their programmes and to inform future directions. Increasingly, universities are recognising the value of using subject- and programme-level student feedback in their quality performance measures as well as integrating the data from their internal feedback surveys with the national surveys to provide a more detailed and multilayered profile of their students' experiences.

References

Abrami, P., d'Apollonia, S. and Rosenfield, S. (2007). 'The dimensionality of student ratings of instruction: an update on what we know, do not know, and need to do'. In R. P. Perry and J C. Smart (eds), *The Scholarship of Teaching and Learning in Higher Education: An Evidence-Based Perspective*. New York: Springer.

Access Economics Pty Ltd (2005). *Review of Higher Education outcome performance indicators*. Report for the Department of Education, Science and Training (DEST). Canberra: Commonwealth Department of Education, Science and Training. Available online at: *http://www.dest.gov.au/sectors/ higher_education/publications_resources/profiles/review_highered_outcome_ perf_indicators.htm* (accessed 23 January 2007).

ACER (2009). *Australasian Survey of Student Engagement* (AUSSE). Available online at: *http://ausse.acer.edu.au* (accessed 22 July 2010).

Asmar, C. (2002). 'Strategies to enhance learning and teaching in a research-extensive university'. *Journal for Academic Development*, 7(1), 18–30.

Australian Quality Agency (AUQA) (2004, 2008). *Cycle 1 and Cycle 2 Audit Handbook*. Available online at: *www.auqa.edu.au* (accessed January 2010).

Barrie, S. and Ginns, P. (2007). 'The linking of national teaching performance indicators to improvements in teaching and learning in classrooms'. *Quality in Higher Education*, 13(3), 275–286.

Barrie, S., Ginns, P. and Prosser, M. (2005). 'Early impact and outcomes of an institutionally aligned, student focused learning perspective on teaching quality assurance'. *Assessment and Evaluation in Higher Education*, 30(6), 641–656.

Barrie, S., Ginns, P. and Symons, R. (2008). *Student surveys on teaching and learning*. Final Report (June). Teaching Quality Indicators Project. ALTC. Available online at: *http://www.altc.edu.au/teaching-quality-indicators* (accessed July 2010).

Bligh, J., Lloyd-Jones, G. and Smith, G. (2000). 'Early effects of a new problem-based clinically oriented curriculum on students' perceptions of teaching'. *Medical Education*, 34, 487–489.

Davies, M., Hirschberg, J., Lye, J. and Johnston, C. (2009). 'A systematic analysis of quality of teaching surveys'. *Assessment and Evaluation in Higher Education*, 35(1), 83–96.

DEEWR (2008). *An Evaluation of the Learning and Teaching Performance Fund*. Department of Education, Employment and Workplace Relations (September). Canberra: Commonwealth of Australia.

DEEWR (2009a). *Transforming Australia's Higher Education System*. Canberra: Commonwealth of Australia. Available online at: *http://www.deewr.gov.au/*

HigherEducation/Pages/TransformingAustraliasHESystem.aspx (accessed 22 July 2010).

DEEWR (2009b). *An indicator framework for higher education performance funding: discussion paper.* December. Available online at: *http://www.deewr. gov.au/HigherEducation/Pages/IndicatorFramework.aspx* (accessed 21 December 2009).

DEST (2004). *Learning and Teaching Performance Fund: Issues Paper.* April. Canberra: Commonwealth of Australia.

DEST (2005). *Learning and Teaching Performance Fund: Future Directions Discussion Paper.* December. Canberra: Commonwealth of Australia.

Edwards, D., Coates, H., Guthrie, B. and Nesteroff, S. (2008). *Postgraduate research experience 2007: the report of the postgraduate research experience questionnaire.* Available online at: *http://works.bepress.com/daniel_edwards/8* (accessed January 2010).

Ewan, C. (2009). *Learning and Teaching in Australian Universities: A thematic analysis of Cycle 1 AUQA audits.* AUQA Occasional Publications Number 18. Australian Universities Quality Agency and the Australian Learning and Teaching Council. June.

GCA (2009). History and development of the AGS. Available online at: *http:// start.graduatecareers.com.au/ags_overview/ags_history_and_development #census* (accessed 8 September 2009).

Krause, K-L., Hartley, R., James, R. and McInnis, C. (2005). *The First Year Experience in Australian Universities: Findings from a Decade of National Studies.* CSHE, University of Melbourne. Available online at: *http://www.cshe. unimelb.edu.au/pdfs/FYEReport05KLK.pdf* (accessed July 2010).

Linke, R.D. (1991). *Performance indicators in higher education: Report of a trial evaluation study, 1.* Canberra: Department of Employment, Education and Training.

Marks, G. and Coates, H. (2007). *Refinement of the Learning and Teaching Performance Fund Adjustment Process.* Report to Department of Education, Science and Training. Melbourne: Australian Council for Educational Research.

Marsh, H.W. (1984). 'Students' evaluations of teaching: Dimensionality, reliability, validity, potential biases and utility'. *Journal of Educational Psychology,* 76, 707–754.

Marsh, H.W. (2007). 'Students' evaluations of university teaching: a multidimensional perspective'. In R.P. Perry and J.C. Smart (eds), *The Scholarship of Teaching and Learning in Higher Education: An Evidence-Based Perspective.* New York: Springer.

Marsh, H. and Cheng, J. (2008). *National Student Survey of Teaching in UK Universities: Preliminary Results.* York: Higher Education Academy. Available online at: *http://www.heacademy.ac.uk/resources/detail/national_student_ survey_of_teachng_in_uk_universities* (accessed 22 July 2010).

Marsh, H.W., Rowe, K. and Martin, A. (2002). 'PhD students' evaluations of research supervision: issues, complexities and challenges in a nationwide Australian experiment in benchmarking universities'. *Journal of Higher Education,* 73(3), 313–348.

McInnis, C., Griffin, P., James, R. and Coates, H. (2001). *Development of the Course Experience Questionnaire (CEQ).* Report funded by Evaluations and

Investigations Programme, Higher Education Division. DETYA, Canberra: Commonwealth of Australia

McKinnon, K.R., Walker, S.H. and Davis, D. (2000). *Benchmarking: A manual for Australian universities.* Canberra: Australian Department of Education, Training and Youth Affairs.

Moses, I. (1988). *Academic staff evaluation and development: a university case study.* Brisbane: University of Queensland Press.

Ramsden, P. (1991). 'A performance indicator of teaching quality in higher education: The Course Experience Questionnaire'. *Studies in Higher Education,* 16 (2), 129–150.

Surridge, P. (2009). *The National Student Survey three years on: What have we learned?* York: Higher Education Academy. Available online at: *http://www. heacademy.ac.uk/ourwork/research/surveys/nss* (accessed January 2010).

Wilson, K., Lizzio, A. and Ramsden, P. (1997). 'The development, validation and application of the Course Experience Questionnaire'. *Studies in Higher Education,* 22(1), 33–53.

Part 3
Tools and administration

Tools for effective student feedback

Hamish Coates

Abstract: Over the last twenty years student feedback data has become an important means of driving quality assurance and improvement in university education. This chapter reviews different kinds of assessments that have been used for this purpose. It begins with an overview of a series of survey instruments. This provides context for investigating the relationship between external and internal assessments, which is undertaken via a range of psychometric analyses. The results of these analyses highlight a number of discontinuities between the instruments used for external and internal quality management. These are explored, and a final concluding section looks at prospects for taking a more considered approach.

Key words: quality enhancement; quality assurance; student feedback tools; survey instruments; student engagement.

An assessment of student feedback instruments

With the rise of the higher education quality assurance agenda over the last few decades, institutions in Australia have sought ways to assess and monitor the quality of teaching. A range of approaches have been considered and implemented, such as peer review and certificate training courses, but the most pervasive quality assurance mechanism would appear to be the development of survey systems to capture student feedback.

A range of different survey systems have been developed. For instance, since the early 1990s Australia has made good use of the nationally administered Course Experience Questionnaire (CEQ) (GCA and ACER, 2009), which is sent to all graduates soon after degree completion.

Institutions have also developed their own subject-specific teaching quality instruments (TQI) for local use in evaluating teaching. Since 2007, a cross-institutional survey of student engagement (the Australasian Survey of Student Engagement, AUSSE) has implemented a Student Engagement Questionnaire (SEQ).

Together, these instruments provide a useful sample of the kinds of feedback mechanisms being used by Australian universities. As such, this chapter concentrates on exploring these instruments, their inter-relationships, and how they are or could be used for quality assurance and enhancement. As this focus suggests, the chapter does not attempt to offer a comprehensive audit of all existing instruments – a very complex exercise and one which many institutions themselves find difficult to produce even for their own internal activities.

The chapter begins with an overview of the three listed assessments – the CEQ, TQI and SEQ. This provides context for investigating the relationship between the CEQ and TQI instruments, which is undertaken via a range of psychometric analyses. The results of these analyses highlight a number of discontinuities between the instruments used for external and internal quality management. These are explored, and the concluding section looks at prospects for a more considered approach.

Overview of selected assessments

Course Experience Questionnaire

Since the early 1990s recent graduates in Australia have been invited to respond to the nationally administered Course Experience Questionnaire (CEQ). This instrument is deployed alongside the Graduate Destination Survey (GDS) around four months after graduation.

The CEQ is designed to probe key elements of the university learning process and, in doing so, obtain data on the quality of teaching. The original CEQ scales were developed with an assumption of a strong association between the quality of student learning and student perceptions of teaching. Working from research conducted on student learning styles in the UK in the 1970s and 1980s (Perry, 1970; Marton and Saljo, 1976; Pask, 1976; Entwistle and Ramsden, 1983), the items and scales are specifically tuned to obtain information on what were considered by Ramsden (1991a) to be the defining elements of teaching and its organisation. By considering the extent to which pedagogy encourages a 'deep' rather than a 'surface' understanding of concepts and materials, the original CEQ attempted to provide a domain-neutral indicator of university course quality. A scale measuring generic skills was added soon after the development of the original CEQ.

A series of new CEQ scales were developed in response to concerns within the higher education community that the original 24-item questionnaire did not examine a sufficiently broad range of aspects of the university student experience. In the late 1990s, research was conducted (McInnis, Griffin, James and Coates, 2001) to expand the existing instrument so as to include other important facets of student experience while retaining the integrity of the existing CEQ. An additional 25 items forming five new scales were introduced in the 2002 questionnaire.

While the current instrument measures 11 facets of the student experience using 49 items, only three scales and 13 'core' items are administered by all institutions. Table 6.1 shows these 13 CEQ items, which in this chapter are henceforth labelled C1 to C13. Together, these provide measurement of 'good teaching', 'generic skills' and 'overall

Table 6.1   Core CEQ items considered in this analysis

Label	Item
C1	The lecturers put a lot of time into commenting on my work
C2	The lecturers normally gave me helpful feedback on how I was going
C3	The lecturers of this course motivated me to do my best work
C4	My lecturers were extremely good at explaining things
C5	The lecturers worked hard to make their subjects interesting
C6	The lecturers made a real effort to understand difficulties I might be having with my work
C7	The course helped me develop my ability to work as a team member
C8	The course sharpened my analytic skills
C9	The course developed my problem-solving skills
C10	The course improved my skills in written communication
C11	As a result of my course, I feel confident about tackling unfamiliar problems
C12	My course helped me to develop the ability to plan my own work
C13	Overall, I was satisfied with the quality of this course

satisfaction', although they also combine psychometrically to measure a single dimension of student satisfaction (Coates, 2007).

All 49 CEQ items share a common response scale. Respondents are asked to express their degree of agreement or disagreement on a five-point scale. By convention, only the 'strongly disagree' and 'strongly agree' points on this scale are labelled on the survey form. In line with the initial development work led by Ramsden (1991b), and the findings of GCCA and ACER (2000) and McInnis et al. (2001), the five-point response categories are interpreted in this report as 'strongly disagree', 'disagree', 'undecided', 'agree' and 'strongly agree'.

Teaching Quality Instruments

To complement the CEQ's lagging, summative and global perspective on the quality of teaching, institutions have developed their own local teaching quality instruments. While several external forces have shaped the formation of institutional survey systems, they have primarily taken shape for the purpose of continuous quality improvement. This context has driven a particular approach to design and delivery. Rather than relying on standard instruments, for instance, each institution has instead developed its own survey forms. Administration strategies have been shaped in line with various institutional policies and practices, and the nature and use made of resulting data has varied considerably across each institution. In general, however, these assessments tend to be administered toward the end of a period of teaching and ask questions about instructional quality and other key facets of institutional support and provision.

A meta-analysis of these TQI was conducted in an attempt to build an integrated understanding of what they are trying to assess (Coates et al., 2010). This involved sourcing TQI items from all Australian public institutions, and transcribing and thematically analysing the items. The thematic analysis built on the earlier research of Davies et al. (2008).

Analysis of the TQI produced a series of broad insights, even before the main analysis had begun. One of the earlier insights was of the vast diversity in the instruments being used, despite the fact that they could all loosely be seen as attempting to measure the same broad phenomena. Further, many of the instruments had clear measurement deficiencies, such as ambiguous or double-barrelled items, unclear response scales, or unclear explanatory statements. While often being deployed for high-stakes use within institutions, critical review of the forms suggests that many would be unlikely to meet quality requirements set by institutional ethics review boards or peer-review research. While no detailed attempt is made here to explain these characteristics, it would appear that they arose due to the non-technical and consensus-driven nature of the development.

After an iterative process of thematic analysis and expert review, the TQI meta-analysis suggested that the instruments attempted to measure the following broad phenomena: clear aims, clear expectations, organisation, teacher enthusiasm, teacher respect for student, access to teachers, teacher knowledge, overall satisfaction, student enthusiasm, stimulating interest, feedback, responsiveness, assessment, student needs, competency development, student encouragement, teaching resources, and workload. As this list suggests, these phenomena tap into diverse and core characteristics of teaching competence and performance. In line with their focus, the instruments did not attempt to measure students' contribution to education outcomes – the extent to which students themselves actively engaged in effective forms of learning and development.

The analysis presented later in this chapter concentrates on TQI items from a sample of four institutions. Together, this sample goes some way to reflect the diversity of items and response formats used across the system, to the extent this is possible. Table 6.2 presents items for each of the four institutions (A, B, D and E) along with their labels. The response categories provided on the survey forms are not shown in Table 6.2, but they are worth noting in order to register their diversity. Specifically:

- University A students are asked to register their responses using a seven-point rating scale of 'strongly disagree', 'disagree', 'mildly disagree', 'undecided', 'mildly agree', 'agree' and 'strongly agree';

- University B students respond using the following scale: 'strongly disagree', 'disagree', 'neither agree nor disagree', 'agree' and 'strongly agree';

- University D's questionnaire uses the same form as University B except that the middle category is labelled 'neutral'; and

- the eight-point University E rating scale is most extensive: 'strongly disagree', 'disagree', 'mildly disagree', 'mildly agree', 'agree', 'strongly agree', 'unable to judge' and 'N/A'.

Table 6.2 Institution-specific TQI items

Label	Item
A1	Activities within the subject provided relevant learning experiences
A2	I understood the concepts presented in this subject
A3	The subject content was presented at an appropriate pace
A4	The subject content was presented at an appropriate level of difficulty
A5	The teaching materials and resources were helpful in directing my learning
A6	Teaching materials and resources were culturally inclusive
A7	This subject helped me develop my thinking skills (e.g. problem solving, analysis)
A8	My ability to work independently has increased
A9	I understood the assessment requirements of the subject
A10	I received useful feedback on my learning
A11	I was able to access quality support (e.g. from lecturers, other students, the university) when appropriate
A12	Overall I was satisfied with the quality of this subject
B1	I had a clear idea of what was expected of me in this subject
B2	This subject was well taught
B3	This subject was intellectually stimulating
B4	I received helpful feedback on how I was going in this subject
B5	In this subject, lecturers showed an interest in the academic needs of the students
B6	I felt part of a group of students and lecturers committed to learning in this subject
B7	There was effective use of computer-based teaching materials in this subject
B8	Web-based materials for this subject were helpful
B9	Overall, I was satisfied with the quality of the learning experience in this subject
D1	The unit addressed the learning outcomes stated in the Unit Outline
D2	The criteria for each assessment component were clearly identified
D3	The workload in this unit was appropriate
D4	There was reasonable opportunity for interaction with lecturers
D5	I was given useful feedback on my assessment work
D6	Submitted work was returned to me in a reasonable time frame

| Table 6.2 | Institution-specific TQI items *(cont'd)* |

D7	The unit stimulated my interest in the subject area
D8	I gained a good understanding of the subject matter
D9	I enhanced my skills in this unit
D10	The unit was well taught
E1	In this subject the learning objectives were made clear to me
E2	The assessment criteria were clearly stated at the beginning of the subject
E3	Feedback on my work was provided to me in time to prepare for other assessment tasks
E4	This subject helped me gain a better understanding of an area of study
E5	My learning in this subject was well supported by access to lecturers
E6	My learning in this subject was well supported by access to other assistance
E7	My learning in this subject was well supported by learning tasks
E8	My learning in this subject was well supported by learning resources
E9	My learning in this subject was well supported by eLearning (if used)
E10	Overall I was satisfied with the quality of this subject

Student Engagement Questionnaire

The Student Engagement Questionnaire (SEQ), developed as part of the Australasian Survey of Student Engagement (AUSSE) (Coates, 2008), was designed to usher in a new way of thinking about education quality in Australian higher education. Rather than focusing on the quality of teaching and service provision, emphasis is placed first on student participation, and then on how institutions are supporting this. It is useful, given this shift in perspective, to provide a brief background on the concept itself.

'Student engagement', broadly considered, is defined as students' involvement with activities and conditions likely to generate high-quality learning and institutions' support of people's involvement (NSSE, 2009; Coates, 2009). The concept, which is clearly central to higher education quality, provides a practical lens for assessing and responding to the significant dynamics, constraints and opportunities facing higher education institutions. It provides key insights into what students are actually doing, a structure for framing conversations about quality, and a stimulus for guiding new thinking about best practice.

Student engagement touches on aspects of teaching, the broader student experience, learners' lives beyond university, and institutional support. It operationalises research that has identified the educational practices linked empirically with high-quality learning and development (see, for instance: Astin, 1979, 1985, 1993; Pace, 1979, 1995; Chickering and Gamson, 1987; Pascarella and Terenzini, 1991). While students are seen to be responsible for constructing their knowledge, learning is also seen to depend on institutions and staff generating conditions that stimulate and encourage involvement.

Surprisingly, given its centrality to education, information on student engagement has only recently been available to Australasian higher education institutions. The AUSSE, conducted with 25 institutions for the first time in 2007, 29 institutions in 2008 and 25 in 2009, provides data that Australian and New Zealand higher education institutions can use to engage students in effective educational practices. Through a licence agreement, the AUSSE builds directly on foundations laid by the North American National Survey of Student Engagement (NSSE, 2009).

The SEQ collects data from institutionally representative samples of first- and later-year students, and provides a foundation for analysing change over time. Although these are not assessments of value added in the statistical sense, examining change across year levels provides insight into the extent to which people are being challenged and pushing themselves to learn. An increase in engagement in active learning practices, for instance, indicates that learners are investing more time constructing new knowledge and understanding. It also indicates that learners are intrinsically more engaged in their work, and hence more likely to be developing their knowledge and skill.

Since 2008, institutions have also had access to a Staff Student Engagement Survey (SSES), which provides a complement to the student collection. The SSES is a survey of academic staff about students, which builds directly on the foundations set by the Faculty Survey of Student Engagement (FSSE) (FSSE, 2009). The Staff Student Engagement Questionnaire (SSEQ) measures academics' expectations for student engagement in educational practices that have been linked empirically with high-quality learning and development. Data is collected from staff, but students remain the unit of analysis.

Compared with student feedback, relatively little information from academic staff is collected in Australasian higher education. The SSES builds on processes developed in recent surveys of staff and leaders

(Coates, Goedegebuure, van der Lee and Meek, 2008; Scott, Coates and Anderson, 2008). Information from staff is important, as it can help identify relationships and gaps between student engagement and staff expectations, and engage staff in discussions about student engagement and in student feedback processes. It can also provide information on staff awareness and perceptions of student learning and enable benchmarking of staff responses across institutions.

The suite of survey instruments – the Student Engagement Questionnaire (SEQ) and the Staff Student Engagement Questionnaire (SSEQ) – that are used in the AUSSE collect information on around 100 specific learning activities and conditions along with information on individual demographics and educational contexts. The instruments contain items that map onto six student engagement scales:

- Academic Challenge – the extent to which expectations and assessments challenge students to learn;
- Active Learning – students' efforts to actively construct knowledge;
- Student and Staff Interactions – the level and nature of students' contact and interaction with teaching staff;
- Enriching Educational Experiences – students' participation in broadening educational activities;
- Supportive Learning Environment – students' feelings of support within the university community; and
- Work Integrated Learning – integration of employment-focused work experiences into study.

The instruments also contain items that map onto seven outcome measures. Average overall grade is captured in a single item, and the other six are composite measures which reflect responses to several items:

- Higher-Order Thinking – participation in higher-order forms of thinking;
- General Learning Outcomes – development of general competencies;
- General Development Outcomes – development of general forms of individual and social development;
- Career Readiness – preparation for participation in the professional workforce;
- Average Overall Grade – average overall grade so far in course;
- Departure Intention – non-graduating students' intentions on not returning to study in the following year; and

- Overall Satisfaction – students' overall satisfaction with their educational experience.

In summary, through the SEQ and SSEQ, the AUSSE provides information about students' intrinsic involvement with their learning, and the extent to which they are making use of available educational opportunities. As such, it offers information on learning processes, is a reliable proxy for learning outcomes, and provides diagnostic measures for learning-enhancement activities. This data can be a powerful means for driving educational change, particularly when linked with feedback from staff.

Connecting the dots: external and internal links

Introduction

Clearly it is essential that there be useful synergies between internal and external quality assessments like those described above. Deliberate triangulation and diversification of information helps strength assessment and review, but it would be counterproductive if evidence from one assessment inadvertently contradicted that of another. This could promote confusion, and might lead to change that in fact resulted in quality reduction rather than improvement.

To explore this matter, the following analysis examines relationships between institution-specific teaching quality instruments (TQI) and the nationally administered Course Experience Questionnaire (CEQ). The analysis was replicated across four universities, each with different TQI items listed in Table 6.2. As noted, in broad terms TQI are designed for continuous improvement while the CEQ is used for summative external evaluation.

This being the case, it is imperative that TQI are empirically aligned with CEQ. If institutions undertake internal improvement activities in response to TQI and these TQI are unaligned with the metrics used for external quality monitoring, then the internal or external systems or their linkages are corrupted. Of course, institutions may look to enhance aspects of education that are not considered by external quality-monitoring activities. But on those measures where there are overlaps, one would expect a relatively high level of relationship. Clearly, it would be counterproductive if institutions enhanced the quality of their teaching and learning and were penalised for this. Equally, it would be perverse if institutions which did not enhance the quality of their teaching received recognition for so doing.

Before comparing scores from the sets of items, it is important to determine whether the items themselves in fact measure the same phenomenon. If institutions' own forms measure different things to those on the CEQ, then driving internal change in ways that register as external improvement could be difficult. The key question is, therefore, whether the institution forms and the CEQ items measure the same constructs.

A series of covariance analyses were conducted to test this proposition. The first looked at whether the CEQ and institution-specific items displayed high levels of consistency when scaled together. The second looked at whether the two groups of items loaded on a single underpinning factor. Finally, confirmatory psychometric modelling was undertaken using Rasch item response modelling to test whether the items provided uni-dimensional measurement of a single construct. This was assessed by reviewing how the items distribute along a single variable, the relative difficulty of each item, and by reviewing mean square statistics which expose the fit of the item to the variable.

In addition to the analysis of construct invariance, a series of analyses were conducted to test the relationship among the CEQ and TQI scale means. While it may make little sense to progress to analysis of the empirical relationship between national and institutional mean scores if the instruments are not measuring the same construct, this relationship is frequently explored in practice and it is worth doing so here. For this, all scale scores were converted into a common reporting metric ranging from 1 to 5.

The analyses below are undertaken within the business field of education. The results are based on 1,022 observations in total. Data was secured by inviting students at four institutions to complete a purposefully designed survey form that contained the 13 CEQ items along with the institution-specific TQI items. In line with the design of the study and data requirements, each analysis was replicated separately for each institution.

Cross-institutional results

Figure 6.1 presents the variable map produced from Rasch analysis of the CEQ and University A items. It shows the distribution of the item demand items on the right-hand side of the variable, and the distribution

Figure 6.1   Variable map: CEQ and University A items

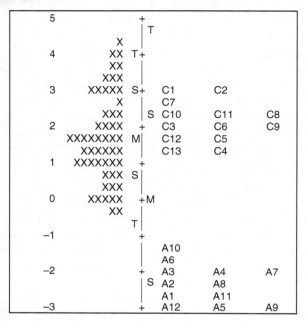

of students' responses on the left-hand side. Review of the item distribution indicates that it is bi-modal, and that the CEQ and university A instruments are largely measuring different constructs. The institution-specific items are considerably 'easier' to agree with than those of the CEQ, and do not appear to scale in an integrated fashion along the common latent variable.

Figure 6.2 shows the mean square fit statistics arising from the Rasch analysis. These have an expected value of 1.0, and figures greater than 1.3 are conventionally read as reflecting a random relationship between the item and latent variable. The CEQ items show good fit to the variable. Many of the institutional items, by contrast, show a loose connection with the variable, particularly item A4, 'The subject content was presented at an appropriate level of difficulty'.

Figure 6.3 charts the relationship between the mean scale scores. The correlation between these was only 0.72. The plot confirms a relatively loose relationship between the external and internal metrics, particularly at the lower end of the distribution.

The presentations given above were repeated for universities B, C, D and E. The results showed that:

Figure 6.2 Fit (mean square): CEQ and University A items

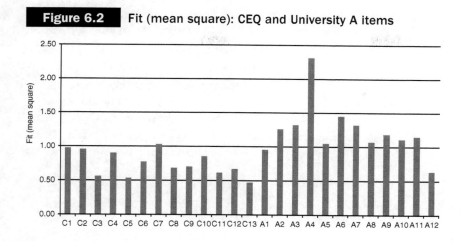

- for University B most of the national and institution-specific items do work together to map out a common underpinning variable, and that the overall relationship between the items is relatively linear;
- the relationship between the CEQ and University D TQI appears relatively robust, although three items do not fit the common variable;

Figure 6.3 Scale mean score relationships: CEQ and University A

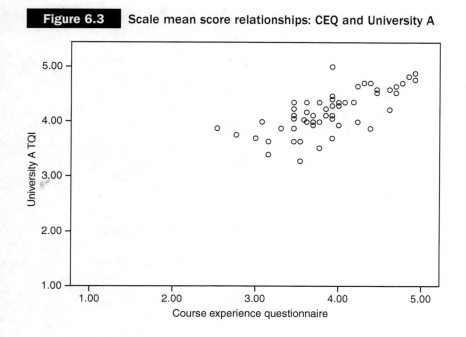

- there appears to be a rough but relatively linear relationship between the CEQ and University D TQI scale means, with the correlation between these being 0.69; and

- items in the University E TQI have the lowest relationship to the CEQ. As with University A, the variable map shows that these items cluster together rather than spreading out to measure a common variable. Almost all of the University E items have mean square fit statistics that lie beyond the acceptable limit of 1.3 – the exceptions are E6, E7, E8 and E10. The correlation between the national and institutional scores is 0.62.

A psychometric disconnect

Overall, these results highlight an alarmingly low level of relationship between the CEQ and TQI. While based on a relatively small amount of evidence, the broad observation holds across various contexts and instruments. There may be several reasons why the CEQ and institutional items appear to measure different constructs.

First, the frame of reference may be different. The institutions' instruments may seek students' perspective on a single subject whereas the CEQ seeks an aggregate perspective on the overall course. In principle, if the instruments are measuring the same constructs, the measurement process should not be confounded by this difference in the level of analysis.

Second, the response scales used by institutions and the CEQ do not align. Variations include the number and labelling of response categories, the presence and positioning of 'not applicable' categories, and the direction of the wording. The direction of wording is likely to introduce most disturbance into the response process, for respondents who complete many such forms may be unlikely to check the precise labelling of the categories before responding. All categories were labelled in a uniform direction for the current analysis, but this alone may have given rise to the response interference effect in question.

Third, and most pointedly, it may be that the instruments do indeed measure different constructs. This is likely given that the instruments were developed at different times for different purposes, and because the institution-specific forms have not been psychometrically validated.

Concluding thoughts on a more considered approach

The above analysis is highly concerning, for it suggests that an institution may be investing considerably to drive continuous improvement in one direction while being prompted to move in another direction by external reinforcement. Ideally, of course, internal and external assessments should be empirically aligned to ensure a non-random relationship between local practice and national estimates of performance.

Developing assessments of student learning that provide sound information to students, institutions and systems remains one of the biggest challenges for higher education. Considerable progress has been made in the last few decades, yet as the above results affirm there are frequent disconnects between the methods used for learning, improvement and accountability purposes. It remains common for classroom practice to play out in completely separate ways to the organisation-level assessments managed by institutional researchers, and for both of these to operate in relative isolation from external quality assurance activities.

There are of course distinct contexts and focuses that shape practice at each of these levels of analysis, yet they share the common basic goal of assessing what learning has been achieved. There would appear to be value, therefore, in identifying approaches that work towards an integration across these levels of analysis. In light of the evidence such as that given above, it is very tempting to consider what productive steps may be taken to align internal and external quality assessments. To this end, this section reviews a new approach being developed with reference to AUSSE, the third assessment considered in this chapter. This involves developing a local version of the external assessment that can help institutions form direct links between local teaching practice and institutional, national and even international performance.

The idea builds on a considerable amount of work undertaken in the USA, and which is scheduled for development and validation in Australasia in 2010. It involves production and use of what, in the USA, has been referred to as the CLASSE (NSSE, 2009). The CLASSE is a class-level adaptation of the USA NSSE, the AUSSE's parent survey (Ouimet and Smallwood, 2005).

The CLASSE is composed of two instruments. As with the SEQ, a student instrument asks students how frequently they participate in effective learning activities within a specific subject. Like the SSEQ, a teacher instrument asks the instructor of that subject how important the defined learning practices are for student success. As with the AUSSE and SSES, student and teacher outcomes can then be contrasted to identify practices that are occurring less frequently than desired or expected. This form of gap analysis provides a highly useful means of stimulating productive change.

Given the results of the analyses above, the advantages of this close integration between internal and external quality assessment instruments are obvious. Subject-level insights about the quality of student engagement can aid instructors' and institutions' efforts to enhance the adoption of engaging educational practices. Framed by institutional or national findings, local results can help spotlight engaging pedagogical practices, shape teaching and learning experiences, and inform staff development activities. The common psychometric thread running through these different levels of analysis – levels which have been hitherto disconnected – provides a firm foundation of evidence for this work.

Our capacity to improve university education hinges in important ways on the technology that is used to define, assess, monitor and enhance core phenomena. This chapter has reviewed key initiatives undertaken in Australian higher education over the last twenty years. It has provided summary descriptions of three different kinds of student feedback instruments, and explored the empirical relationships between those used widely in Australia for quality assurance and continuous improvement for some time. Review of the instruments, and results from this analysis, implied that a new more strategic approach to aligning the assessment of university education could facilitate more advanced forms of assessment and improvement. As suggested by way of conclusion, finding better ways to link how learners, teachers, institutions and systems use feedback information to improve remains a core challenge for research and practice.

References

Astin, A.W. (1979). *Four Critical Years: Effects of college on beliefs, attitudes and knowledge.* San Francisco: Jossey-Bass.

Astin, A.W. (1985). *Achieving Educational Excellence: A critical analysis of priorities and practices in higher education.* San Francisco: Jossey-Bass.

Astin, A.W. (1993). *What Matters in College: Four critical years revisited.* San Francisco: Jossey-Bass.

Chickering, A.W. and Gamson, Z.F. (1987). 'Seven principles for good practice in undergraduate education'. *AAHE Bulletin*, 39(7), 3–7.

Coates, H. (2007). 'Universities on the catwalk: models for performance ranking in Australia'. *Higher Education Management and Policy*, 19(2), 1–17.

Coates, H. (2008). *Attracting, Engaging and Retaining: New conversations about learning. Australasian Student Engagement Report.* Camberwell, Australia: Australian Council for Educational Research.

Coates, H. (2009). 'Development of the Australasian Survey of Student Engagement (AUSSE)'. *Higher Education*, 60(1), 1–17.

Coates, H., Goedegebuure, L., van der Lee, J. and Meek, L. (2008). 'The Australian academic profession: a first overview'. *Report of the International Conference on the Changing Academic Profession Project, 2008.* Hiroshima University: Research Institute for Higher Education.

Coates, H. Hirschberg, J. and Lye, J. (2010). The matching of quality of teaching indicators and the Course Experience Questionnaire. Paper presented at the 15th Australasian Teaching Economics Conference, Hamilton, New Zealand.

Davies, M., Hirschberg, J., Lye, J. and Johnston, C. (2008). 'A systematic analysis of quality of teaching surveys'. *Department of Economics Working Papers Series 1050.* University of Melbourne.

Entwistle, N.J. and Ramsden, P. (1983). *Understanding Student Learning.* Manuka: Croom Helm Australia.

Faculty Survey of Student Engagement (FNSSE) (2009). *Faculty Survey of Student Engagement (FSSE).* Available online at: *http://nsse.iub.edu* (accessed 1 February 2009).

GCA and ACER (2009). *Graduate Course Experience, 2008: The Report of the Course Experience Questionnaire.* Parkville, Australia: GCA.

GCCA and ACER (2000). *1999 Course Experience Questionnaire.* Melbourne, Australia: GCCA.

Marton, F. and Saljo, R. (1976). 'On qualitative differences in learning: outcome as a function of the learner's conception of the task'. *British Journal of Educational Psychology*, 46, 4–11.

McInnis, C., Griffin, P., James, R.H. and Coates, H.B. (2001). *Development of the Course Experience Questionnaire.* Canberra, Australia: Department of Employment, Training and Youth Affairs.

National Survey of Student Engagement (NSSE). (2009). *National Survey of Student Engagement (NSSE).* Available online at: *http://nsse.iub.edu* (accessed 1 February 2009).

Ouimet, J.A. and Smallwood, R.A. (2005). 'Assessment measures: CLASSE – the class-level survey of student engagement'. *Assessment Update*, 17(6), 13–15.

Pace, C.R. (1979). *Measuring Outcomes of College: Fifty years of findings and recommendations for the future.* San Francisco: Jossey-Bass.

Pace, C.R. (1995). *From good practices to good products: Relating good practices in undergraduate education to student achievement.* Paper presented at the Association for Institutional Research, Boston, USA.

Pascarella, E.T. and Terenzini, P.T. (1991). *How College Affects Students: Findings and insights from twenty years of research.* San Francisco: Jossey-Bass.

Pask, G. (1976). 'Conversational techniques in the study and practice of education'. *British Journal of Educational Psychology*, 46, 12–25.

Perry, W.G. (1970). *Forms of Intellectual and Ethical Development in the College Years: A scheme.* New York: Holt, Rinehart & Winston.

Ramsden, P. (1991a). 'A performance indicator of teaching quality in higher education: The Course Experience Questionnaire'. *Studies in Higher Education*, 16(2), 129–150.

Ramsden, P. (1991b). 'Report on the CEQ trial'. In R. Linke (ed.), *Performance Indicators in Higher Education Volume 2*. Canberra, Australia: Australian Government Publishing Service.

Scott, G., Coates, H. and Anderson, M. (2008). *Learning leaders in times of change: Academic leadership capabilities for Australian higher education*. Sydney, Australia: Carrick Institute for Learning and Teaching in Higher Education.

Web-based or paper-based surveys: a quandary?

Lorraine Bennett and Chenicheri Sid Nair

Abstract: Over the last decade, the routine collection of stakeholder feedback has gradually become embedded in university quality systems throughout Australia. The most common practice is the use of surveys to evaluate student perceptions of their units (subjects), course (programme) and overall student experience. Initially, most surveys were paper-based and administered in class. Over time, web-based surveys have been introduced and while it is accepted that this survey mode delivers administrative efficiencies, a widespread view is that students are less likely to respond to web-based surveys. This chapter tests this assumption by examining the usage patterns of print-based and web-based student unit evaluation surveys and response rate trends over a period of three years at a large research-intensive university in Australia. While this analysis is restricted to one university's data, it points to some important findings for leaders in other universities who are responsible for making decisions about quality assurance policies, practices and budgets.

Key words: student surveys; web-based surveys; paper-based surveys; evaluation; response rates.

Introduction

With the growth of quality assurance in universities and an emphasis on quality of teaching and accountability, there has been a parallel growth in implementing effective stakeholder feedback mechanisms. Bennett and Nair (2010) reported that this significant increase is underpinned by four drivers: diagnostic feedback to aid in the development and improvement of teaching; research data to inform design changes in units, courses, curriculum and teaching; administrative decision-making activities (e.g. performance management and development appraisals); information for current and potential students in the selection of units and courses; and measurement of the quality of units and courses that is increasingly tied to external funding sources and formulas.

Stakeholder feedback is primarily collected by surveys utilising traditional paper-based administration and, more recently, online administration. This trend was documented in a study of American universities conducted in 2003 which suggested that around 45 per cent of universities are either actively engaged with web-based surveys, considering the use of web-based instruments or have planned to initiate web-based feedback in the next round of evaluations (Hoffman, 2003). This change is significant when compared to a study reported three years earlier by Hmieleski and Champagne (2000) where the data suggested online usage for surveys in universities was around 2 per cent.

One possible explanation for this increase in online surveys is that learning environments are more flexible than previously, which in turn requires the evaluation systems to keep pace with the change. Students increasingly have more flexibility in how, where and when they study and the requirement to attend class is largely disappearing in the new global learning environment. Utilisation of web-based surveys is also linked to an increase in the take-up rates of mobile digital communication devices. As society, and students in particular, becomes more reliant and comfortable with iPhones, personal tablets, laptops and other mobile devices, they prefer many of their routine interactions with the university to be conducted online. Despite the popularity of mobile digital devices, the use of web-based surveys has met with resistance, especially from some academic staff, who cited low response rates and unreliability of results as reasons for their concerns (e.g. Dommeyer et al., 2004).

This chapter examines web-based surveys from the point of view of administration, response rates and usefulness of student feedback. Trend data from a large Australian research-intensive university, which used both print-based and web-based surveys over a three-year period, are analysed. The findings provide some valuable observations on paper-based and web-based survey tools for institutions and university leaders. The findings also highlighted the need for further research on the use of paper-based and web-based survey tools across other universities in order to investigate whether the findings from this single case can be generalised to the wider higher education sector.

Administrative considerations

Practice and data strongly support the view that administration of web-based surveys has many advantages over administration of print-based surveys. Some of these advantages include:

- *Cost.* Although web-based approaches may initially require large development costs, the operational costs are relatively low compared with print-based systems. The savings come from not having to print questionnaires, especially high-quality questionnaires suitable for optical scanning. There are also considerable savings from not having to employ staff to distribute, collect, clean questionnaires for scanning, scan, transcribe comments, re-enter responses on damaged questionnaires and to store data (Bennett and Nair, 2010; Dommeyer et al., 2004; Bothell and Henderson, 2003; Johnson, 2003).

- *Class time.* Web-based surveys are typically not conducted during class time, unlike print-based surveys, thus web-based surveys do not infringe on valuable time set aside for teaching (Dommeyer et al., 2004; Sorenson and Reiner, 2003).

- *Accessibility.* Many surveys are administered near the end of the term when some participants are absent from the classroom. The availability of surveys online allows greater opportunity for participants to complete them at a time when it suits them (Ardalan et al., 2007).

- *Data processing and storage.* With online collection, the data are processed as soon as they are entered. There is also less need to clean the data collected online (Dommeyer et al., 2004; Sorenson and Reiner, 2003). Unlike paper-based surveys which are bulky to store, web-based surveys can be stored electronically, which also makes them easier to retrieve.

- *Anonymity and confidentiality.* Compared to paper surveys, online surveys have a distinct advantage in that participant handwriting does not appear on completed questionnaires. Although this ensures student anonymity, as pointed out by Dommeyer et al. (2004), other studies have indicated that anonymity is still an issue as log-ins can be matched to individual students via the student management systems (Avery et al., 2006).

- *Provide more information.* Researchers comparing online and paper-based responses have shown that participants provide more information to open-ended questions in an online environment compared to paper-based format (Ardalan et al., 2007; Dommeyer et al., 2004; Hmieleski and Champagne, 2000; Layne, DeCristoforo and McGinty, 1999).

Further, an added advantage of most online tools is that they allow participants to return to their responses and edit them before final submission.

■ *Freedom to provide feedback without external influence.* Dommeyer et al. (2004) argued that in web-based surveys there is less opportunity for faculty or other interested parties to influence the evaluation. Further, research literature also asserts that the presence of the teacher in or near the classroom when questionnaires are administered in-class can impact on the evaluation outcome (Ardalan et al., 2007).

■ *One response per participant.* Another advantage of web-based surveys over paper-based surveys is that safeguards can be built in to prevent multiple completions of surveys by a single participant.

■ *Closing the loop.* With a faster turn-around time in producing reports, which is facilitated by web-based surveys, it is possible to enable participants in the surveys to view their feedback at the same time these reports are viewed by teachers, managers and administrators.

The previous discussion has identified many administrative advantages of web-based surveys. However, a key disadvantage that is often cited in literature is that online responses typically elicit lower response rates than 'in-class' administration of surveys (Dommeyer et al., 2004; Porter, 2004). The issue of response rates with respect to print and web-based surveys is investigated in the following section.

Survey response rates

Several studies have suggested possible reasons for low response rates to web-based surveys. The reasons ranged from the fear that student responses can be tracked back through to student apathy and technical impediments (Avery et al., 2006; Dommeyer et al., 2004; Sorenson and Reiner, 2003). The type of technical barriers raised included: low levels of computer literacy among certain cohorts; slow modem speeds; unreliable internet connections; low-end or outdated browsers; limited accessibility to computers at convenient times for the students to complete and submit the surveys; and other accessibility problems, in particular for disabled students (Dommeyer et al., 2004; Cummings et al., 2001; Ravelli, 2000; Sorenson and Reiner, 2003).

However, current thinking suggests that low response rates are more likely due to the lack of engagement of students in the process than technical issues (Coates, 2006; Nair et al., 2008). Consequently, a variety of strategies designed to encourage greater student participation have been explored in the literature. These include: systematic reminder emails; the practice of requiring students to complete surveys before they can get access to online registration of new courses or obtain other information from the institution's web pages; and the use of enticements to elicit greater interest from potential respondents (Coates et al., 2006; Dommeyer et al., 2004; Porter, 2004). The evidence on incentives has been somewhat varied, with no indication that an incentive always results in a higher response rate (Dommeyer et al., 2004). Major disadvantages and ethical questions in having incentives have also been identified. These included, for instance, the cost of reasonable incentives according to the needs of the cohort and the compliance with international gambling laws (Bennett and Nair, 2010).

While the above studies may point to some factors which contribute to low response rates, there is an emerging view that low response rates are highly correlated to a lack of follow-up action. In other words, response rates are generally quite low where there is little evidence of action being taken in response to feedback (Harvey, 2003; Leckey and Neil, 2001; Powney and Hall, 1998). Leckey and Neil (2001) argued that 'closing the loop' is an important issue in terms of total quality management: 'If students do not see any actions resulting from their feedback, they may become sceptical and unwilling to participate' (p. 25). Harvey (2003) supported this finding, adding that students need to be convinced that change has occurred based on their feedback. Bennett and Nair (2010) also suggested that there was a need to provide more information to students about the purposes and the subsequent use of evaluations in the quality process.

Naturally, those who are involved in analysis and discussion of survey results are interested in response rates and the difference between web- and print-based surveys. However, several studies reported that there was little evidence to suggest that online surveys with lower response rates produce biased evaluations (Coates et al., 2006; Layne et al., 1999; Porter, 2004). Other studies which looked at the difference between online versus paper-based surveys showed similar mean scores, factor structures and reliabilities (Buchanan and Smith, 1999; Fouladi et al., 2002).

Bennett and Nair (2010) reported similar findings in a study carried out at an Australian research-intensive university on unit evaluation data for first-year Business and Economics students. In this study, the initial online survey was re-run in a paper-based format. The response rate for the paper-based survey was 65 per cent and for the online survey 36 per cent. The differences in the results for items relating to the overall unit were not found to be statistically significant. The conclusion from this work was that the generic results from the unit evaluation questionnaire were reliable, despite the smaller sample size for online surveys compared to the print-based surveys.

Analysis of trend data

The previous section of this chapter documented growth in web-based surveys across the higher education sector and discussed the administrative benefits of this mode of collecting student feedback. It also challenged perceived concerns of the effects of lower response rates on the reliability of the feedback. The next section explores these discussions further by analysing trend data from a large research-intensive Australian university which has administered both print-based and web-based surveys for over three years.

The university has more than 55,000 students. It operates across six Australian and two international campuses in Malaysia and South Africa and offers many courses in partnerships in other countries including Singapore, Hong Kong and Indonesia. The data utilised are from student unit (subject) evaluations, which is the core quality feedback tool administered at the university. The unit evaluation survey contains ten core items common to all unit evaluations with up to ten additional quantitative items nominated by a faculty. The surveys are administered each semester but each unit is evaluated at least once in the year it is offered.

In 2005, the institution invested significantly in implementing a state-of-the-art electronic evaluation system, which facilitates both online and paper-based administration of surveys (Nair and Wayland, 2005). The evaluation system has a number of advantages, including the ability to store all data in a central database as well as providing accessibility of surveys to the visually handicapped.

Online unit evaluations are administrated over a five-week period towards the end of each semester. Paper-based evaluations are administered on a schedule developed by faculties and usually conducted during the last week of each semester. Administrators other than the instructors oversee the completion of surveys during class time. On average, a typical full-time student would be asked to complete four evaluations each semester.

Students in units selected to be electronically evaluated are notified by e-mail at the start of the five-week period. The evaluations are accessed through the student portal, which is linked to the relevant unit evaluation questionnaires. Students completing web-based evaluations can complete the survey at the time of their choice within the five-week period. Reminder e-mails are sent weekly to students who have not responded. Students are advised in the e-mails that their responses remain anonymous and confidential and their student identity is not linked to their responses in the database. Results of the student evaluation of units are posted on a common website for all staff and students to review at the end of the survey period.

Results

Student evaluations of units are undertaken for each unit, in the year they are offered. Table 7.1 summarises the number of units that were evaluated using the web and paper-based modes of administration for the years 2006, 2007 and 2008. The decrease in the overall number of units evaluated from 2006 (8,243) to 2008 (7,698) is a result of a major review of units offered during this time. The number of units evaluated in 2009 was 5,926 (semester one).

Figure 7.1 tracks the usage pathways for print-based and web-based surveys. It illustrates the decrease in the number of web-based surveys between 2006 with over 80 per cent to about 58 per cent in 2008. It shows paper-based surveys as a mirror image of the web-based trends. Although the full data for 2009 was not yet available at the time of writing this chapter, early indicators suggest that the trend to increased print-based and reduced web-based surveys in 2007 and 2008 will be reversed in 2009, where a greater preference for web-based surveys has

Table 7.1 Number of units evaluated, 2006–2008

Year	Size of potential responses	Number of units evaluated		
		Web	Paper	Total
2006	283,575	6,902	1,341	8,243
2007	293,827	5,575	2,912	8,487
2008	293,784	4,441	3,257	7,698

Figure 7.1 Evaluation mode trends

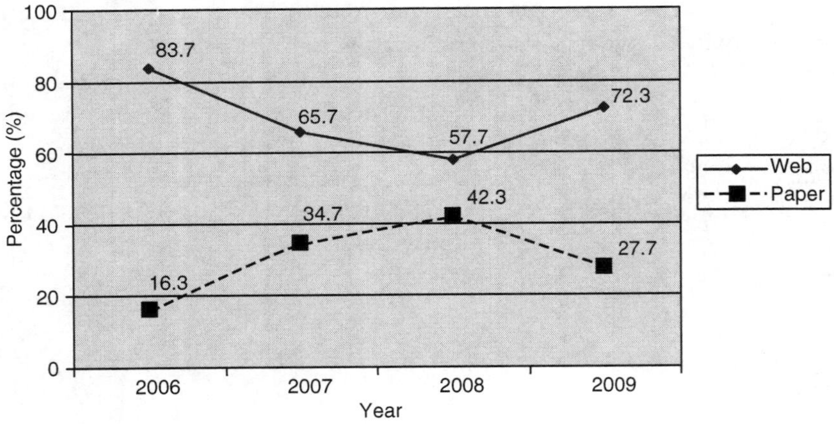

re-emerged (web-based surveys for semester one stand at around 72 per cent; see Figure 7.1).

The data on response rates for web-based and print-based surveys also reveal some notable trends. Firstly, there was a gradual increase in overall response rates for unit evaluation surveys. Table 7.2 indicates a steady climb from 38.2 per cent in 2006 to 50.2 per cent in 2008. Another noteworthy aspect to point out is that while paper-based response rates reached a plateau around the mid to low 50 per cent, the response rate for web-based surveys has grown from 30.8 per cent in 2006 to 40.6 per cent in 2008.

Table 7.2 Response rates, 2006–2008 (percentages)

Year	Number of units evaluated		
	Web	Paper	Total
2006	30.8	55.1	38.2
2007	33.8	53.5	44.9
2008	40.6	53.4	50.2

Discussion

The data presented in this chapter suggested that in 2006 there was a remarkably high preference (over 80 per cent) for web-based evaluation surveys among academic staff, which contradicts the concerns about low response rates and subsequent unreliability of the data reported in the literature. This suggests that staff and decision-makers at this university were either unaware of the literature or felt that the advantages of web-based administration of surveys outweighed the concerns. It may also reflect a staff profile which is technologically informed and attuned to student communication preferences and technology usage patterns.

Although the demand for web-based surveys in the university declined from 2006 to 2008, the number of web-based surveys requested was still very strong, with over 4,441 units (57.6 per cent) evaluated using a web-based survey in 2008. In addition, the data available for 2009 semester one suggest a strong swing to web-based surveys with around 72.2 per cent of units nominated for web-based administration.

The data on response rates for web-based and print-based surveys revealed some noteworthy trends. The overall response rate increased from 38.2 per cent in 2006 to over 50 per cent in 2008, while the total number of units evaluated and the population size remained fairly constant. These figures would appear to diminish the fears of those who promote theories of the so-called 'survey fatigue'. This evidence strongly suggests that students were still willing to complete surveys, and indeed participation was growing rather than diminishing.

The response rate for the print-based surveys over the period was around 53 per cent, while the web-based response rate improved by 10 per cent (from 30.8 per cent to 40.6 per cent). This trend of web-based evaluations yielding higher response rates over time supports Avery et al.'s (2006) findings. Interestingly, like other studies, such as Dommeyer et al. (2004), which suggested utilising incentives to boost participation rates, the unit evaluation process described in this study did not utilise any form of incentives except the approach of informing students that their feedback will be used for improvements and students will be informed of the changes (Bennett and Nair, 2010).

The data analysed in this study support other research findings that suggest that web-based surveys are likely to produce lower response rates than traditional paper-based methods. The reasons for the higher response rates for paper-based surveys reported in the literature tend to be centred on the benefits of having a captive audience in the classroom, where there is little competition for the attention or time of the student. Furthermore, there is a view that higher response rates in the surveys administered in the classroom may be a result of the influence of instructors in class requesting that the evaluations be filled out. On the other hand, web-based evaluations are usually completed in one's own time, in the personal space of the respondent, and are not subject to pressures to respond which may be present in the classroom environment.

Table 7.2 suggests that response rates for paper-based surveys have reached a plateau. There are a number of possible reasons for this flattening out. On average, a student completes four unit evaluations at the end of each semester, along with other teacher evaluations. Class observations conducted by these authors indicate that students were often not able to distinguish between teacher and unit evaluations, which resulted in some students' not responding to a second questionnaire in the same class. Another plausible explanation is that in the current higher education environment many students do not attend class regularly because of work commitments and the availability of learning materials online. Instructors have reported this growing trend as a reason for lower than expected response rates in paper-based surveys. Online surveys, on the other hand, have shown a steady increase (see Table 7.2).

The authors are aware that this chapter draws conclusions based on data from a single institution. Therefore, further research is needed to investigate the wider applicability of the findings regarding the increase in online survey response rates presented here. There are a number of factors which should, however, be noted. Firstly, current students are more attuned to electronic forms of surveying, thus the cohorts are more technology-savvy. Secondly, a number of units have online components which make it very convenient for students to complete web-based surveys, as they work online on a regular basis. Thirdly, online surveys have a distinct advantage of enabling participants to complete the survey at a time and place of their choosing. This sits well with the current student cohort, where many students not only take online units but are also frequently off-campus due to employment and family commitments. Further, there is greater acceptance that web-based surveys provide a confidential and anonymous way to give feedback.

Staff in higher education institutions are often critical about online surveys. This is often based on an assumption that online surveys tend to produce significantly fewer responses than paper-based surveys. Table 7.2 indicates that this gap may be closing and is likely to continue to reduce as web-based surveys become more embedded in the higher education system. The work of Bennett and Nair (2010) suggests that implementation of effective communication and engagement strategies is effective in increasing student participation rates. Such strategies include regular communication with students on the use of survey data, assuring the student body that the surveys are confidential and anonymous and demonstrating that student feedback is used to initiate change by providing specific examples of improvements.

The findings reported in this study need to be viewed within the following limitations. Firstly, the data reported on in this study was drawn from one university and only relates to student unit (subject) evaluations. Secondly, no formal student interviews were conducted to explore possible reasons for the generally lower but steadily increasing response rates for web-based surveys. Further, research is required to delve into the reasons behind the growing popularity of web-based surveys. The use of student focus groups may be one way of further investigating the dynamics of web-based surveys.

Conclusions

University leaders and quality managers are acutely aware of the need to listen regularly to the student voice. Evaluation surveys are one of the most popular ways of routinely collecting student feedback, and the decision whether to use print-based or web-based surveys – or indeed a combination of both – is a constant challenge. In many cases, low response rates from web-based surveys limit the use of data that has been collected. The findings presented in this chapter suggest that web-based evaluations are not only an effective form of surveying students but that there is a tendency of response rates increasing over time.

Similarly to other research findings, this study found that web-based evaluation methods (compared to paper-based approaches) produced lower response rates. However, the evidence in this chapter suggests that web-based surveys still provide valuable information and that, over time, they are likely to yield higher response rates due to student preferences for mobile and digital methods of communication.

While further research is required to test this assumption, the authors are of the view that, at the case study university, practical changes in the way web-based surveys were administered (including a strategic communication plan) led to increases in response rates. This chapter suggests that, to increase web-based survey response rates, it is important to engage with stakeholders in the media of their choice.

References

Ardalan, A., Ardalan, R., Coppage, S. and Crouch, W. (2007). 'A comparison of student feedback obtained through paper-based and web-based surveys of faculty teaching'. *British Journal of Educational Technology*, 38(6), 1085–1101.

Avery, R.J., Bryan, W.K., Mathios, A., Kang, H. and Bell, D. (2006). 'Electronic course evaluations: Does an online delivery system influence student evaluations?' *Journal of Economic Education*, 37(1), 21–37.

Bennett, L. and Nair, C.S. (2010), 'A recipe for effective participation rates for web-based surveys'. *Assessment and Evaluation in Higher Education*, 35(4), 357–365. Available online at: *http://pdfserve.informaworld.com/347850_751308601_913269474.pdf* (accessed February 2010).

Bothell, T.W. and Henderson, T. (2003). 'Do online ratings of instruction make sense?' In D.L. Sorenson and T.D. Johnson (Eds.), 'Online student ratings of instruction'. *New Directions for Teaching and Learning*, 96, 69–80.

Buchanan, T. and Smith, J.L. (1999). 'Using the Internet for psychological research: Personality testing on the World Wide Web'. *British Journal of Psychology*, 90, 125–144.

Coates, H. (2006). 'Student engagement in campus-based and online education'. *University connections*. London: Taylor & Francis.

Coates, H., Tilbrook, C., Guthrie, B. and Bryant, G. (2006). *Enhancing the GCA National Surveys: An examination of critical factors leading to enhancements in the instrument, methodology and process.* Canberra, Australia: Department of Education, Science and Training.

Cummings, R., Ballantyne, C. and Fowler, L. (2001). 'Online student feedback surveys: encouraging staff and student use'. In E. Santhanam (ed.), *Student Feedback on Teaching: Reflections and Projections, Refereed Proceedings of Teaching Evaluation Forum*, 29–37. Crawley, Australia: University of Western Australia. Available online at: *http://www.csd.uwa.edu.au/spot/forum/forum_monograph.pdf* (accessed May 2010).

Dommeyer, C.J., Baum, P., Hanna, R.W. and Chapman, K.S. (2004). 'Gathering faculty teaching evaluations by in-class and online surveys: their effects on response rates and evaluations'. *Assessment and Evaluation in Higher Education*, 29(5), 611–623.

Fouladi, R.T., McCarthy, C.J. and Moller, N.P. (2002). 'Paper-and-pencil or online? Evaluating mode effects on measures of emotional functioning and attachment'. *Assessment*, 9, 204–215.

Harvey, L. (2003). 'Student Feedback'. *Quality in Higher Education*, 9(1), 3–20.

Hmieleski, K. and Champagne, M.V. (2000). 'Plugging into course evaluation'. *The Technology Source*, Sept/Oct. Available online at: *http://technologysource.org/article/plugging_in_to_course_evaluation/* (accessed March 2010).

Hoffman, K.M. (2003). 'Online course evaluations and reporting in higher education'. In D.L. Sorenson and T.D. Johnson (eds), 'Online student ratings of instruction'. *New Directions for Teaching and Learning*, 96, 25–30.

Johnson, T.D. (2003). 'Online student ratings: will students respond?'. In D.L. Sorenson and T.D. Johnson (eds), 'Online student ratings of instruction'. *New Directions for Teaching and Learning*, 96, 49–60.

Layne, B. H., DeCristoforo, J.R. and McGinty, D.(1999). 'Electronic versus traditional student ratings of instruction'. *Research in Higher Education*, 40(2), 221–232.

Leckey, J. and Neill, N. (2001). 'Quantifying quality: the importance of student feedback'. *Quality in Higher Education*, 7(1), 19–32.

Nair, C.S., Adams, P. and Mertova, P. (2008). 'Student engagement: the key to improving survey response rates'. *Quality in Higher Education*, 14 (3), 225–232.

Nair, C.S. and Wayland, C. (2005). 'Quality and evaluation: a universal system for a quality outcome'. *Engaging Communities: Proceedings of the Australian Universities Quality Forum*. Melbourne, Australia: Australian Universities Quality Agency, pp. 127–130.

Porter, S.R. (ed.) (2004). *Overcoming Survey Research Problems*. San Francisco: Jossey-Bass.

Powney, J. and Hall, J. (1998). *Closing the Loop: The impact of student feedback on students; subsequent learning*. Edinburgh: Scottish Council for Research in Education.

Ravelli, B. (2000). *Anonymous Online Teaching Assessments: Preliminary Findings*. Available online at: *http://eric.ed.gov/PDFS/ED445069.pdf* (accessed July 2010).

Sorenson, D.L. and Reiner, C. (2003). 'Charting the uncharted seas of online student ratings of instruction'. In D.L. Sorenson and T.D. Johnson (eds), 'Online student ratings of instruction'. *New Directions for Teaching and Learning*, 96, 1–24.

Inclusive practice in student feedback systems

Chenicheri Sid Nair, Phillip Adams and Patricie Mertova

Abstract: Web-based or online surveys in general have a number of advantages in terms of the ease of administration, data collection and storage, resulting in financial and time savings. Despite these advantages, the usual shortfall to such surveys hosted on the web has been the generally lower response rates. This chapter initiates a discussion concerning inclusive practice in student feedback systems. It outlines a case of a research-intensive university which moved towards online administration of its surveys with the introduction of a new Survey Management System (SMS).

Key words: evaluation; inclusive practice; quality; platform; online surveys.

Introduction

Students are among the most important stakeholders for any university and yet for many years universities did not take seriously into account their views of the teaching and learning environment. Further, over the years, the student landscape has experienced significant shifts, creating fundamental changes to the student population. Students now display much more varied levels of academic, cultural and linguistic preparation for tertiary study. They also exhibit a more diverse range of expectations and needs.

With the growth of the quality assurance process in universities and an emphasis on the quality of teaching and accountability, there has been an increase in the implementation of effective stakeholder feedback mechanisms. Although paper administration has been the mode most often utilised in the past to elicit such feedback, the trend in universities is to opt for online administration. Hoffam (2003), in a study of US universities, suggested that around 45 per cent of universities are either actively engaged with online surveys, considering the use of online instruments or have planned to initiate online feedback in the next round of evaluations. When this study is compared to an earlier review reported by Hmieleski and Champagne (2000), the data suggested online usage for surveys in universities was hovering around just 2 per cent. A possible reasoning for this increase is that learning environments in universities are more flexible than they used to be, which in turn requires the evaluation systems to keep pace with the change. Students currently have the flexibility in how, where and when they study. In other words, the requirement to attend class is no longer a prerequisite in the new global learning environment.

Literature outlines numerous advantages of web-based surveys when compared to paper administration. A list of such advantages is outlined in Chapter 7 (see 'Administrative considerations').

Although there are many advantages which support the use of online administration, a key disadvantage that is often cited in the literature is that online responses typically elicit lower response rates than 'in-class' administration of surveys (e.g. Dommeyer et al., 2004; Porter, 2004). Literature cites numerous possibilities of why online response rates are low. This ranges from the fear of students concerning the possibility of tracking their responses, student apathy and technical issues (e.g. Avery et al., 2006; Dommeyer et al., 2004; Sorenson and Reiner, 2003). Researchers suggest many reasons relating to technical issues. These include the low levels of computer literacy among certain participant cohorts, slow connection speeds, low-end or outdated browsers, lack of accessibility to computers at convenient times for the students to complete and submit the surveys, and accessibility problems in particular for disabled students (Dommeyer et al., 2004; Cummings et al., 2001; Ravelli, 2000; Sorenson and Reiner, 2003).

A contributing factor to response rate, though not significant, is the participation of the visually impaired in online surveys. Although literature points to difficulties faced by the visually impaired in using the Internet and the development of tools to help in their accessibility (e.g. Macias and Sanchez, 2001; Murphy et al., 2007; Leporini et al., 2004), little has been reported on how institutions tailor their evaluation system to allow for the effective participation of these students.

However, more recent research suggests that low responses are generally due to the lack of engagement of stakeholders in the process (Coates,

2006; Nair et al., 2008). A variety of strategies have been explored in literature and include systematic reminder e-mails, 'forcing' students to complete surveys prior to online registration of courses or obtaining other information from the institution's web pages and the possibility of enticements in the form of incentives to elicit greater interest from potential respondents (e.g. Coates et al., 2006; Dommeyer et al., 2004; Porter, 2004).

Generally, response rates are pivotal when survey results are discussed. A thorough discussion on the factors effecting and the importance of response rates is provided in Chapter 7.

In general, feedback from stakeholders is considered critical in a good-quality system. With this importance and the increasing demand for undertaking continuous improvement, the emphasis has been on obtaining feedback from a spectrum of activities in universities. A factor that has always been discussed at institutions is that, for evaluation data to be of value, response rates need to be sufficiently high to be representative of the stakeholder cohort. This chapter describes how the central quality unit within one large Australian research-intensive university identified a technical issue that potentially limited the responses of students who completed the semester unit (subject) evaluations via online surveys. The technical change was first applied to unit evaluation surveys and then expanded to apply to all online surveys hosted by the university's survey management system.

Institutional approach to unit evaluation

The university described in this chapter is a large research-intensive and highly internationalised institution which is home to more than 55,000 students from around 130 countries. The diversity of the university's operation is reflected in its activities across six Australian and two international campuses (in Malaysia and South Africa), and it offers many courses in partnerships in countries such as Singapore, Hong Kong and Indonesia.

Units or subjects are the vital 'building blocks' of the curriculum in any university. For this university, the importance of embedding a systematic way of monitoring units was identified as a major recommendation in the institutional self-review *Still Learning* in 2002 (Monash University, 2002).

The policy governing unit (subject) evaluation was developed in 1998 and revised in 2005. Two stages are identifiable up to 2005. Prior to

2002, unit evaluation was conducted mostly utilising an item bank system where academics created their own unit questionnaires from a selection of over 100 items in the item bank. This produced a system where academics took ownership of the timing of evaluation and the reports produced were usually in a singular aggregated format for individual units. The second stage, introduced in 2002, saw a shift of responsibility from the academic to the faculty. In this stage, faculties were required to design a common faculty-wide questionnaire and to conduct an evaluation of each unit at least every five years. This second stage saw a patchy uptake by faculties, resulting in a mixture of both processes in this period. This gave rise to a broad combination of questions which did not provide a way to benchmark or to monitor and improve units within the university. Further, the results of the surveys were not always available within the faculty for review.

In 2005, a new evaluation system was approved by the Academic Board, which had significant operational and design changes. These included:

- ten core items common to all unit evaluations across the university;
- the addition of up to ten quantitative items by a faculty in order to produce a report common to the faculty;
- student evaluation to be undertaken of each unit each year they were offered;
- results of the student evaluation of units posted on a common website for all staff and students to review;
- results from the evaluations to be systematically considered by faculties in each semester with reporting to a central committee on the improvements.

With this significant shift in policy and demand, the university invested sizeable resources in re-engineering the technology to back the increasing need for data in the monitoring stage of the quality life cycle. To facilitate the administration of the survey, the university's central quality unit introduced a new Survey Management System (SMS), replacing the legacy system that used optical scanning technology. The new SMS system allowed for the first time either paper-based or online surveys for all units to be processed. The software utilised in the SMS was chosen to line up with the university's commitment to inclusive principles as spelled out in the Inclusive and Practice Disability Plan:

> The aim of the Plan is to achieve universal accessibility mainly by ensuring that all planning (including the physical, learning,

teaching, research and IT) identifies and eliminates barriers to participation of all people including those who have a disability. Monash University (2004)

Discussion

At the time of the implementation of the new SMS system at the university, web-based questionnaires for unit evaluation were produced in the Portable Document Format (PDF). This format allowed participants to view the survey instrument as a PDF document, while giving them the ability to fill it in without downloading. PDF formatting was inherent to the SMS, which was part of the commercially available tool introduced at the university. This type of format, although appealing in its presentation, was found to be 'clumsy' in its practical application, evidenced by the numerous issues that were raised by the students. In the first year of administration, 157 students or about 0.3 per cent of students surveyed took the time to lodge their dissatisfaction (see Figure 8.1). A similar number of students reported issues in the second year (108 students or just around 0.2 per cent of those surveyed). Anecdotal evidence by faculties suggests the numbers of students having difficulty accessing the PDF were significantly higher.

Further, students who were visually handicapped highlighted their inability to complete surveys online, although the software was one that

Figure 8.1   Unit evaluation online access complaints 2005–2008

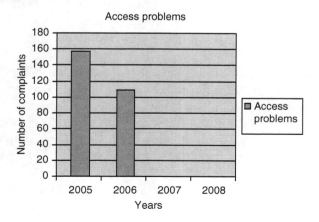

had passed compliance with survey development for the visually impaired. A concern was raised by visually impaired students that the PDF format was not accessible when using screen readers and was not user-friendly. Visually handicapped students wishing to complete online surveys had to first identify themselves and, following this, an evaluation team member would provide one-to-one assistance to complete the evaluation. This was initially accomplished by reading the questions to the students, usually over the phone, and completing the online survey on their behalf. Later, surveys were customised to utilise screen readers. These approaches were individually-based solutions that required visually impaired students to identify themselves, thus compromising their anonymity and failing to support the principles of inclusive practice.

In general, students raised a numbers of areas of concern in accessing this type of survey. These included the unfamiliarity with PDF documents being fillable online, which resulted in many students downloading the form and trying to submit their responses. The following comment is representative of the concerns.

> I am having trouble completing the online unit evaluations. I can open the PDF file, but once there I can't select the options that I want. This is the second time that I have tried, so not sure what is wrong?

Furthermore, this difficulty was supported by a number of students forwarding a printed form of their response to the central quality unit to lodge their feedback.

The second concern related to incompatibilities of some versions of the browser used by the students to access the survey. To compound this problem, some areas of the university also had older versions of the browser that did not allow access for students, even though they were using university machines. The following comments are indicative of these concerns:

> I am unable to click the response in the questionnaire. I am sure that I access the evaluation forms by using Internet Explorer 6.0 and Adobe Reader 7.0. I also set Adobe Reader to display PDF forms in the browser. Please help me. (Student 1)
>
> I attempted to complete this form; however, I got an error message – something to do with my web browser. (Student 2)

Finally, the set-up of the web browser that required the PDF to be displayed within a browser window was raised by a number of students. To assist the students to correct the display, requiring them to adjust control panel settings, step-by-step instructions were sent to those with problems.

During the first two years of the surveys, these issues of accessibility were lodged repeatedly by students. The new evaluation process ensured that every student had the opportunity to provide feedback. As a result of these concerns, the survey platform utilised in the new SMS system was altered to deliver the online questionnaire in HyperText Markup Language (HTML) format, designed using a survey tool specifically developed to be compliant with the World Wide Web Consortium (W3C) accessibility standards. The tool was developed entirely within the university using freely available source code and only functionality that conformed to accessibility standards.

This change was trialled with visually handicapped students, prior to being introduced as the new platform for all surveys. Feedback from these student trials was positive, particularly in that it could be read using any of the screen readers available and was presented in a clear and logical format and, consequently, that it was easy to complete for these students. Working with an expert in accessibility standards, the system was designed to meet all requirements of W3C. This also included the design of a wide variety of question types, with each type being carefully assessed to ensure that it was fully accessible for all students.

Information from other Australian universities suggests that the change in technology illustrated in this chapter to include all participants in the process, especially those with disabilities, places the university at the forefront of applying inclusive practice in the evaluations area. All online surveys hosted by the university now bear the Web Content Accessibility Guideline (WCAG) Conformance logo in line with the W3C requirements.

The change had two significant results. First, there were no complaints from students on using the online questionnaire (see Figure 8.1), and second, there has been a significant increase in web-based responses from 30.8 per cent to 41.6 per cent. Despite this, the overall survey response rate only showed around a four percentage point increase after the first year of implementation. A possible reason as to why the response rate did not increase more significantly was that students who had used the system prior to the change had not returned to complete the surveys the following year because of their negative experiences with the evaluation system. Although other factors (such as an effective communication strategy with the students, engagement of students and staff in the survey process and survey item design) play a part in the increase in response rate (e.g.

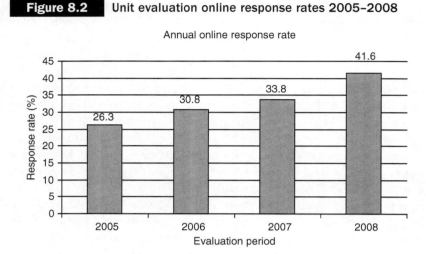

Figure 8.2 Unit evaluation online response rates 2005–2008

Annual online response rate

Bennett and Nair, 2010; Nair et al., 2008), the contention of this chapter is that the change of the presentation platform had a positive impact to assist in the rise in response rate (see Figure 8.2) and is a factor that needs consideration in web-based surveys.

Concluding remarks

The results suggest that feedback from students relating to the tool that is utilised for surveys is critical to the success of online evaluations. This is in line with earlier studies that suggest surveys that are easily and readily accessible and easy to use are valued by students (e.g. Dommeyer et al., 2004; Layne et al., 1999; Ravelli, 2000). These studies further report that if students run into technology-related issues, or they have difficulty in navigating the system or do not understand how the system operates, they are less likely to complete the web-based surveys. This was apparent in the initial system that was implemented at the large Australian university, where students were reluctant to return to the site to complete the surveys when they had difficulty understanding and using the PDF format of the questionnaire. Further, it was also resource-intensive for the university's central quality unit to resolve each issue raised by students on an individual basis.

The driving force for the change in the system was the realisation that students with disabilities, especially those who were visually impaired, were excluded from the evaluation process because of the incompatibility of the technology (screen readers) they were utilising to access these surveys. This limitation in the system also worked against the university's desire to give all students the opportunity to provide confidential and anonymous feedback when surveyed.

This chapter has underlined the idea that all institutions have a duty of care to enable all their students to access and provide feedback to the institutional surveys, thus enabling an inclusive evaluation system that does not discriminate among its key stakeholders. Addressing the needs of all students would therefore further the progress of equity and fairness within the university community. The chapter has further highlighted the fact that any quality system employed at an institution must consider the effectiveness of the evaluation system that is employed at the institution. To this effect, it needs to take on board the feedback from its stakeholders and improve the services they provide by changing the process so as to accommodate the needs of all its stakeholders. The data from the university presented here suggest that students found a change of platform for web-based questionnaires in the institution user-friendly, which in turn had a positive influence on response rates.

In summary, a system that is inclusive of the needs of all stakeholders reinforces the notion that all stakeholders are of equal importance, which in turn sends a message of inclusivity in the feedback process.

References

Avery, R.J., Bryan, W.K., Mathios, A., Kang, H. and Bell, D. (2006). 'Electronic course evaluations: does an online delivery system influence student evaluations?', *Journal of Economic Education*, 37(1), 21–37.

Bennett, L. and Nair, C.S. (2010). 'A recipe for effective participation rates for web based surveys', *Assessment and Evaluation in Higher Education*, 35(4), 357–365.

Coates, H. (2006). *Student Engagement in Campus-based and Online Education University connections*. London: Taylor & Francis.

Coates, H., Tilbrook, C., Guthrie, B. and Bryant, G. (2006). *Enhancing the GCA National Surveys: An examination of critical factors leading to enhancements in the instrument, methodology and process*. Canberra, Australia: Department of Education, Science and Training.

Cummings, R., Ballantyne, C. and Fowler, L. (2000). 'Online student feedback surveys: encouraging staff and student use'. In E. Santhanam (ed.), *Student Feedback on Teaching: Reflections and Projections, Refereed Proceedings of Teaching Evaluation Forum*, 29–37. Crawley: University of Western Australia. Available online at: *http://www.csd.uwa.edu.au/spot/forum/forum_monograph.pdf* (accessed February 2010).

Dommeyer, C.J., Baum, P., Hanna, R.W. and Chapman, K.S. (2004). 'Gathering faculty teaching evaluations by in-class and online surveys: their effects on response rates and evaluations'. *Assessment & Evaluation in Higher Education*, 29(5), 611–623.

Hmieleski, K. and Champagne, M.V. (2000). 'Plugging into course evalaution', *The Technology Source, Sept/Oct.* Available online at: *http://technologysource. org/article/plugging_in_to_course_evaluation/* (accessed February 2010).

Hoffman, K.M. (2003). 'Online course evaluations and reporting in higher education'. In D.L. Sorenson and T.D. Johnson (eds), 'Online student ratings of instruction', *New Directions for Teaching and Learning, 96*, 25–30.

Layne, B.H., DeCristoforo, J.R. and McGinty, D. (1999). 'Electronic versus traditional student ratings of instruction'. *Research in Higher Education*, 40(2), 221–232.

Leporini, B., Andronico, P. and Buzzi, M. (2004). *Designing search engine user interface for the visually impaired*. Proceedings of the 2004 international cross-disciplinary workshop on web accessibility (W4A), 57–66. Available online at: *http://portal.acm.org/citation.cfm?id=990668* (accessed 20 August 2009).

Macias, M. and Sanchez, F. (2001). *Improving Web accessibility for visually handicapped people using KAI*. Proceedings of the 3rd International Workshop on Web Site Evolution, 49–54. Available online at: *http://ieeexplore.ieee. org/stamp/stamp.jsp?tp=&arnumber=988785&isnumber=21298* (accessed 20 August 2009).

Monash University. (2002). *Still Learning: The Report of our Self-Review.* Available online at: *http://www.adm.monash.edu.au/cheq/reviews/still-learning/ contents.html* (accessed February 2010).

Monash University. (2004). *Inclusive Practices: Disability Plan 2004–2008.* Available onlilne at: *http://www.adm.monash.edu/sss/equity-diversity/disability-liaison/inclusive-practices-plan.html* (accessed 21 August 2009).

Murphy, E., Kuber, R. McAllister, G., Strain, P. and Yu W. (2007). 'An empirical investigation into the difficulties experienced by visually impaired Internet users.' *Universal Access in the Information Society*, 7(1–2), 79–91.

Nair, C.S., Adams, P. and Mertova, P. (2008). 'Student engagement: the key to imporving survey response rates'. *Quality in Higher Education*, 14 (3), 225–232.

Porter, S.R. (ed.) (2004). *Overcoming Survey Research Problems.* San Francisco: Jossey-Bass.

Ravelli, B. (2000). *Anonymous Online Teaching Assessments: Preliminary Findings.* Available at: *http://eric.ed.gov/PDFS/ED445069.pdf* (accessed July 2010).

Sorenson, D.L. and Reiner, C. (2003). 'Charting the uncharted seas of online student ratings of instruction'. In D.L. Sorenson and T.D. Johnson (eds), 'Online student ratings of instruction', *New Directions for Teaching and Learning, 96*, 1–24.

Action and the feedback cycle

James Williams

Abstract: Most higher education institutions now assiduously collect feedback from their students and many produce large and detailed reports (Harvey, 2003). However, it is much less clear how this process results in action and how information on such action is fed back to the students themselves. These two final elements of the feedback cycle are distinct but both vital in making the feedback cycle effective and, most importantly, in engaging the students with the feedback process (Powney and Hall, 1998; Leckey and Neill, 2001). This chapter first explores action processes at a number of institutions that use the Student Satisfaction Approach. Second, the chapter explores the different ways in which institutions feed information on such action back to their students, building on early work by Watson (2003). At these institutions, there is a commitment to taking action as a result of student feedback and the feedback process is closely integrated into the institutional management structure. Action has become a necessary part of the institutional calendar. However, closing the feedback loop is more problematic: institutions use a variety of ways of communicating with their students but there is little agreement on what is most effective.

Key words: feedback cycle; action; expectations; management; ownership; improvement.

Introduction

Although much has been written about the collection of students' feedback on their experiences of higher education (Richardson, 2005), an assumption appears to be made that it is valuable in its own right. One of the most common concerns expressed by students in discussion is that the time they spend in completing questionnaires is wasted because nothing is done as a result. For these students, therefore, institutional claims that student views matter, or that the student voice is listened to, are nullified by the lack of any visible action. It is, therefore, not merely necessary for student feedback to be collected; it is essential that transparent action takes place as a result.

Although a causal link between action and feedback is difficult to prove, it is clear that a rise in satisfaction with an item often coincides with action as a result of regular, annual student feedback surveys. Existing student feedback survey reports indicate that where student data has been used to inform improvement, this has had a direct impact on resulting student satisfaction. Satisfaction, Williams and Kane (2008; 2009) argued, is therefore a dynamic process that depends on institutions asking for feedback from their students and acting upon the information. Furthermore, students need to be made aware of the action that has been taken so that they can see that the feedback process is worthwhile and not merely an empty gesture.

Harvey (2003) argued that student feedback is a cyclical process. First, student input, gained through group feedback processes (Green et al., 1994) and from comments they made on the previous year's survey, feed into the questionnaire design process. Second, the questionnaire is distributed, returned, scanned and the data analysed. Third, the resulting report feeds into senior management quality improvement processes and action is taken. Finally, action is reported back to the students, who are then again asked for input into the questionnaire design process (see Figure 9.1).

This cycle is a fundamental element of the *Student Satisfaction Approach* (Harvey et al., 1997). This flexible methodology for collecting and using student feedback was developed at the University of Central England during the 1990s and has been used here and at a large number of higher education institutions in the UK and around the world, and consequently provides a large set of data on student experience and actions taken as a result (Williams and Kane, 2008). This chapter is largely based on data that has been collected as part of the 'Student Satisfaction' process because the data is largely comparable.

Action

Feedback and action have long been linked theoretically. Harvey et al. (1997, part 10: 5) argued that the Student Satisfaction approach 'requires

Figure 9.1 The student feedback/action cycle

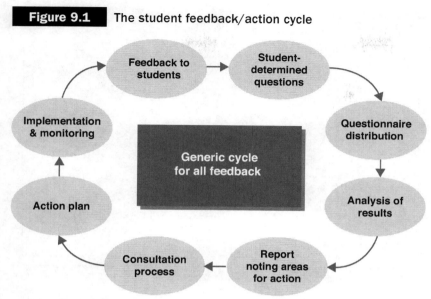

Source: Harvey L., (2003).

senior institutional managers and divisional managers to ensure that action is taken to address areas of concern'. Leckey and Neill (2001) argued from their experience at the University of Ulster that student evaluation 'if addressed properly, . . . is a formal acknowledgement by an institution that it respects student views when taking account of both setting and monitoring standards' (p. 29). It is a long-standing principle of evaluation that action is taken as a result of canvassing stakeholder experience (Harvey, 1998).

In practice, when an institution takes clear and effective action, satisfaction scores often rise. The two processes are not coincidental: the satisfaction process is a dynamic one and is intended to be so. The results in consequent student satisfaction can sometimes be very clear when presented in longitudinal graphs. For example, satisfaction with an aspect of the university's computing facilities, and the availability of Internet access, increased across the faculties at the University of Central England (UCE) over the period 1998 to 2007 (Figure 9.2) and the changes correspond to action taken by the university over the same period.

The graph in Figure 9.2 is particularly illuminating because it shows a significant rise in satisfaction with the item on Internet access over the period 1996 to 2000. In 1996, the item was introduced into the questionnaire and it elicited very low satisfaction levels. In 1997, the item

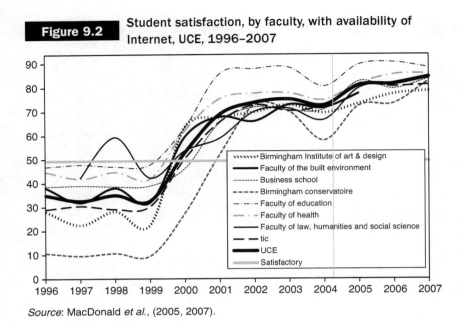

Figure 9.2 Student satisfaction, by faculty, with availability of Internet, UCE, 1996–2007

Source: MacDonald *et al.*, (2005, 2007).

again received low satisfaction. As a response, in 1998, the university stated that it was in the process of connecting all faculties to the Internet. One faculty, Law, Humanities and Social Science, was stated to have 'invested in IT facilities and has a ten-computer room with access to the Internet and email. A further 20 stations with Internet access are currently being set up' (Aston et al., 1998: 17). It is noticeable in Figure 9.2 that satisfaction levels from Law, Humanities and Social Sciences rose significantly in 1998. The following year, 1999, there was a drop in satisfaction levels, and as a result, further action was taken which focused resources on the faculties that were regarded as unsatisfactory and, as a consequence, significant sums were allocated to extend e-mail operations across the University (Blackwell et al., 1999: 16).[1]

In 2000, satisfaction was rising, but the focus of university action remained on the Conservatoire and the Technology Innovation Centre (*tic*, formerly Faculty of Engineering and Computer Technology) as access to the Internet in these faculties was still regarded as unsatisfactory. As a result of poor scores in the 1999 survey, facilities were expanded (Bowes et al., 2000).

Thereafter, satisfaction with the availability of the Internet continued to rise, and as a result, the issue ceased to appear in the action section of the annual report. Significant action by the university was reflected in increased levels of student satisfaction.

However, action cannot always be clear, immediate and dramatically visible in improvement of student satisfaction. Many student concerns are long-term and the responses can only be long-term. A good example of this is the institutional response to assessment and feedback on students' work. In the UK's National Student Survey (NSS), shock was expressed by the media and government at the relatively poor performance in two items, the 'usefulness of lecturers' feedback on my work' and the 'promptness of tutors'/lecturers' feedback on my work'. These two areas have, for many years, been known by commentators and institutions to be difficult to improve. An exploration of student satisfaction data over 15 years showed that in institutions which have run a detailed Student Satisfaction Survey, predating the limited NSS, satisfaction has increased over time as action has been taken (Williams and Kane, 2008). Satisfaction levels to date, although not high (usually in the region of 50 to 60 per cent), have increased significantly in institutions where tailored satisfaction surveys were instituted. For example, this can be seen clearly in the case of UCE (Figure 9.3).

Assessment and feedback is often mentioned in institutional feedback to staff and students as an area in which action is being taken. At UCE, 'the issue of promptness of feedback on assignments has always been very important to students and satisfaction varies from faculty to faculty and from course to course' (Bowes et al., 2000: 11).

Figure 9.3 Student perceptions of usefulness and promptness of feedback, UCE, 1996–2007

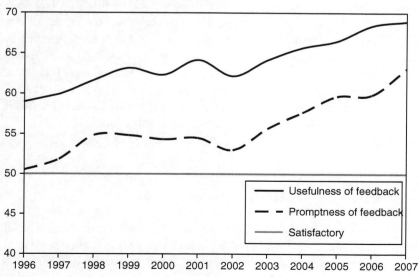

Publicly available feedback information at UCE demonstrates that the issue of feedback as it is raised by students has been addressed by management in several different ways since the mid 1990s. Faculties that have scored badly on assessment issues have responded by setting realistic targets for assignment turnaround and, importantly, made assessment and feedback schedules clearer to their students. In 1995–96, for example, UCE instituted more realistic turnaround targets:

> In response [to low satisfaction with promptness of feedback] the faculty [of Computing and Information Studies] set a target of a 'four-working-week turnaround' on assignments, which has proved very successful. (Geall et al., 1996)

At Sheffield Hallam University, there was a 'three-week rule' for the return of feedback to students (Sheffield Hallam University, 2003), although it has been made clear, publicly, that this is difficult to achieve in some faculties. Communication is a consistent feature of action.

Responses to institutional surveys largely fall into two categories. First, the institution clarifies its procedures to the students. Second, the institution recognises that it can improve its own processes.

Real action vs no real action

In the cases highlighted above, action has been taken in response to student concerns. However, it is not always clear what action has been taken in reality. Such 'actions' include announcements that issues will be discussed at an indeterminate point in the future. Although this indicates that issues have not been ignored, the survey has little impact if it is not followed up by definite action. Not only does the lack of action limit the impact of the satisfaction survey process, it arguably has a negative impact on the process as students lose faith in it. As Leckey and Neill (2001) argue, 'feedback is of little use, indeed it is of negative value, if it is not addressed appropriately' (p. 29).

Monitoring action

Monitoring is necessary to ensure that effective action is taken and followed through. It is necessary to ensure that real action is developed from faculty- or university-level meetings but it is also necessary to make sure that action that has been started is followed through. Too often, in student satisfaction reports, action may be described but there is little information about how it is followed through.

Monitoring is now common, with action particularly on assessment and feedback, arguably because of the near panic engendered by the National Student Survey. However, a common response to issues raised by student satisfaction surveys has long been to institute an effective monitoring system. Different faculties at UCE, for example, used different approaches. In the Faculty of Education, in 2005–06, monitoring of the timing and placing of assessments was carried out in order to make improvements in this area (MacDonald et al., 2006). In the Faculty of Engineering in 1998–99, selected modules were audited and students were specifically asked to comment on this issue. The Board of Studies was charged with determining those modules where promptness of feedback was a problem (Blackwell et al., 1999). In addition, some faculties instituted systems to track student coursework to ensure that feedback is provided according to schedules.

Managing student expectations

A common concern raised amongst practitioners is that student satisfaction surveys may be raising unrealistic expectations among students. However, it is important not to let this deflect researchers and managers from the real purpose of student surveys, which is to gather and hear the student voice. It is important not to pose questions that raise expectations about issues over which an institution has little or no control (for example, car parking) and focus on items that are within the institution's remit. Nevertheless, it is vital to treat the student voice, as expressed through surveys, with respect and not simply to 'manage' student expectations. If a key part of the feedback process is action, then it is vital to respect what the students are saying.

What might be described as 'unrealistic expectations' about facilities may in reality be an issue of appropriate training in the use of those facilities. For example, student concerns that there are not enough books relevant to their course in the library may not be a false expectation but it might also be that they have not been given enough training in the use of library resources. This might, therefore, involve further discussions with staff and students about what is necessary for students to get more out of their experience of the library. At UCE, following poor library scores for the ease of locating books on the shelves and for other items in 2002 (see Figure 9.4), a series of focus groups were held with staff and students from the Faculty of Law and Social Sciences. This was aimed at identifying the main areas of concern. The discussions led to a report and the designation of adequate funding to addressing stock concerns. Over the summer period, the library carried out an extensive programme of renewal and replacement of its stock and in following years the satisfaction level rose dramatically (MacDonald et al., 2003).

In addition, the library's large-scale refurbishment programme, carried out over the period from 2005 to 2007, significantly improved the appearance, user-friendliness and content of the library, all of which may have contributed to general satisfaction with library items in the annual student satisfaction survey.

Another example related to realistic or unrealistic expectations is the issue of the promptness of tutors' feedback on students' work. The institutional response should not be aimed at 'managing student expectations'; rather it should be about making clear what is possible and what is relevant to the students. For instance, it may be true that lecturers cannot provide feedback within two weeks when they have several

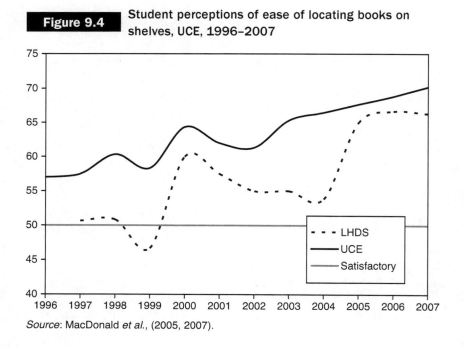

Figure 9.4 Student perceptions of ease of locating books on shelves, UCE, 1996–2007

Source: MacDonald *et al.*, (2005, 2007).

hundred papers to mark, let alone other duties to perform. This is entirely understandable; however, it does not help the students if they need the feedback for an assignment that follows shortly afterwards. An argument is then necessary for a change in the timetabling of assignments rather than an increased burden on the lecturers. Indeed, as Williams and Kane found (2008: 67), 'ensuring an even spread of assessments is one approach that has been used by institutions'. At the UCE, over the period 2005–07, attempts were made to spread assignments more evenly by changing the teaching programme (MacDonald et al., 2007).

Some institutions are finding that the assessment load on their students is too great and have taken measures to reduce it. The response from at least one UK university has been to change courses from a 15- to a 20-credit framework (Williams and Kane, 2008). This is reflected in the wider discussion about assessment – modular structures have led to shorter courses and, as a result, more frequent assessment (Gibbs, 2006).

Students' ownership of the feedback process

There remains, however, little direct evidence that students are more likely to complete questionnaires as a result of knowing that action is taken as a result of their participation. Experience suggests that surveys tend to attract larger numbers of respondents when the purpose is clear and action results.

A brief scan of comments from students at three universities relating directly to their institutional satisfaction questionnaires showed, that in the majority of cases where there were comments, the concern is with the size or relevance of the questionnaire.[2] However, there were several comments that showed a deeper engagement with the overall purpose of the survey process.

Some comments were positive and recognised that the questionnaire process is a valuable method of improving the institution. The following comments reflect this view:

> Questionnaire is a good idea so the University can try and improve even more. (Student 1, University B, 2007).

> This questionnaire is an excellent idea since it is impossible for the management to just guess what the students are pleased with or having difficulties as well. (Student 2, University A, 2006).

Questionnaire is spot on highlighting relevant importance of how the points of the course should be structured and followed through consistently. This can improve both performances between staff and students. (Student 3, University A, 2007).

Some comments demonstrated a degree of cynicism about the process. These students argued that the process is not about real action but about fulfilling requirements. The following comments reflect this view:

If it would make a difference I would fill it in. This is an exercise to be seen to be doing the right thing. (Student 1, University A, 2007).

Does any of this feedback actually get acted upon? (Student 2, University C, 2009).

Some students believe that the survey is a pointless exercise because they can see no action resulting from completing the questionnaire annually:

This would be the third questionnaire I have completed. There has been no response to the complaints raised by way of the questionnaire or as a result of writing to the Vice Chancellor direct. And pretty pointless. (Student 1, University A, 2007).

I usually relish the opportunity to give feedback as it is a very important tool. However, it needs to be relevant to the participant and not take up so much time. (Student 2, University A, 2007).

Tell us what exactly you have done having received these feedbacks instead of repeatedly sending so many questionnaire forms with a cheap 25 pound lure. (Student 3, University C, 2009).

Interestingly, one student felt that the survey process would be better operated by the students themselves in order to make it more relevant:

This questionnaire is better handled by students with more/adequate knowledge of the university as a whole, i.e. students who have been on the campus for up to or over one year. (Student 1, University A, 2006).

Such a view has merit and student ownership occurs, for example, at Lund University in Sweden and in some UK universities, such as the

University of Bath, where the student satisfaction survey was established 'as a partnership between the University of Bath and the Students' Union as part of the University of Bath's Learning and Teaching Strategy' (University of Bath, 2009). It is interesting to note that the University of Bath achieves a relatively high response rate compared with other UK institutions, indicating a potentially important role for the Students' Union in the feedback process.

Feedback to students

Actions taken as a result of a student satisfaction survey need to be fed back to the students to make it clear that their voice is listened to. Harvey et al. (1997) claimed that such 'feedback is not only a courtesy to those who have taken the time to respond but it is also essential to demonstrate that the process both identifies areas of student concern and does something about them'. Leckey and Neil (2001) argued that what is important is what is done with this student input, namely: 'what action is taken; how the outcomes are conveyed to the students themselves' (p. 31).

In their study *Closing the Loop*, Powney and Hall (1998) found that students were less likely to take ownership of the student feedback process or even the wider quality improvement process if they were unaware of action that resulted. Richardson (2005) argued that students are more likely to be sceptical about the value of taking ownership of feedback processes where little institutional response is visible:

> Many students and teachers believe that student feedback is useful and informative, but many teachers and institutions do not take student feedback sufficiently seriously. The main issues are: the interpretation of feedback; institutional reward structures; the publication of feedback; and a sense of ownership of feedback on the part of both teachers and students. (p. 410)

This is a difficult issue and many institutions have tried different approaches over the last twenty years with varying degrees of success.

At its simplest, feedback can be provided through a detailed leaflet. For example, at the UCE, a four-page feedback flyer, *Update*, was developed, which outlined the main actions that were taken by the university and faculties as a result of the survey. This was based on the principles laid out by Harvey et al. (1997). The leaflet was distributed with the following year's questionnaire in order both to inform the students of actions taken as a result of the survey and to encourage students to complete the new survey. Other institutions have followed this model: Auckland University of Technology, New Zealand, University of Technology Sydney (UTS), Australia, and Lincoln University and the University of Greenwich in England have all produced substantial newsletters detailing action as a result of their student satisfaction surveys (Watson, 2003).

A shorter, glossier approach is sometimes thought to be more effective in catching the student's eye. At Sheffield Hallam University, a 'glossy, marketing-type leaflet' (Watson, 2003: 151) was produced in 2002–03, outlining the main action outcomes of the student satisfaction survey. A similar approach was taken at 'Midland University'. Key actions across the university are summarised in a glossy, colourful one-page leaflet. As in the UCE model, this is distributed with the following year's questionnaire in order to encourage students to complete the survey and demonstrate that action has resulted since the previous year.

These examples are paper-based, but other institutions use a range of different media to present the message that action has been taken. Bulletin boards, student websites and student radio have all been used to broadcast the message that student feedback is acted upon. This approach has been used by the University of Portsmouth and by Sheffield Hallam University as a way of supporting the paper leaflet. UTS was considering placing an item in the 'What's New' section of their home page and sending batched emails outlining results to their students (Watson, 2003). Sheffield Hallam University sent a short e-mail to all students with just the headline issue that had been implemented as a result of the last Student Satisfaction Survey, with a link to a more detailed account of changes. This was just prior to the invitation to complete the current year's survey.

As Watson found (2003), a further channel for feeding back information on action is through direct communication with students. Two universities in the UK in Watson's study used student representative fora to disseminate information. Another university forwarded the student experience report and resulting action memoranda to the students' association. However, this approach relies upon student representatives forwarding this information to their peers. At Lund University in Sweden, the students are closely involved in the process and results of that University's Student Barometer (*Lärobarometern*) are discussed with the students at a special conference (Nilsson, 2001).

Students' perspectives on the feedback flyer

However, it is unclear how effective different feedback methods are and this is another area in which further research would be useful. At University A in March 2007, a small project was carried out to collect views on the efficacy of the feedback flyer. The following comments suggested that the flyer was considered rather dull and unappealing:

> Seen but not read because it's boring. (Student 1)

> Boring, only interested in the iPod [the participant prize], didn't like the letter from directorate, no colour, grey, need more pictures, don't recognise it as a letter, doesn't appeal to the eye, more summaries, looks like a dull newspaper article, looks like a political leaflet. (Student 2)

The following comments suggest that the paper-format of a flyer is dull, and that it would be better presented on the Internet in a more personal manner:

> Colourful, creative, more diagrams, more eye-catching, prefer to receive it by email, on a website, combine it with a newsletter, personalised letter. (Student 1)

> Seeing the results happen, put feedback notices where applicable, email findings to the university email accounts, eye-catching video or link to faculty websites, put it on moodle [University virtual learning environment]. (Student 2)

Conclusions

The material covered in this chapter indicates, above all, that if an institution takes real action on the basis of what its students tell it through large-scale institutional feedback surveys and makes it clear that action has been taken, satisfaction increases over time. Institutional feedback surveys, therefore, fulfil the long-standing and core principle of survey development that action is taken as a result of canvassing stakeholder opinion.

It is vital that real action is taken and seen to be taken, otherwise students are disillusioned with the survey process. It is important that institutions ensure, through effective monitoring processes, that real action is taken. Institutions must not view the survey process simply as an exercise in 'managing expectations': students are not 'customers' but principal stakeholders whose voice provides direct and valuable data on their experience. Many issues raised by students are not solved by attempts to reduce their expectations but by working with students and within what is realistic for all stakeholders, including academic staff.

As part of the courtesy to students for taking time to complete questionnaires, it is necessary to make it clear to them that action has been taken. The survey process thus has a clear purpose of which respondents are aware. In order to make this process more effective, further research is necessary into the nature of student responses to institutional student feedback surveys and how students respond to feedback information about action.

A commitment to a methodology such as the Student Satisfaction Approach, it is argued (Harvey, 1997), is principally the result of an institution recognising that certain aspects of the student experience require improvement and that listening and acting upon the students' own experience through regular feedback surveys is one way of doing so. This is a mature approach to informing change but, arguably, recent responses to the NSS in the UK are more concerned with appearing well in another set of league tables than committing to a robust and transparent quality (feedback) cycle.

Notes

1. Although there is no clear evidence from the data or existing (published) reports to explain this phenomenon, experience suggests that it is quite common for satisfaction levels to drop noticeably following an initial rise. Arguably, this may be explained by increased demand following initial outlay or by a failure of an institution to keep up concerted action.
2. The three UK institutions have been anonymised because the student comments from the questionnaires largely remain unpublished. University A is a large metropolitan institution which was formerly a polytechnic. University B is a medium-sized former polytechnic. University C is a small out-of-town campus university founded in the 1960s.

References

Aston, J., Blackwell, A., Williamson, E., Williams, A., Harvey, L., Plimmer, L., Bowes, L., Moon, S. and Owen, B. (1998). *The 1998 Report on the Student Experience at UCE*. Birmingham: University of Central England.

Blackwell, A., Harvey, L., Bowes, L., Williamson, E., Lane, C., Howard, C., Marlow-Hayes, N., Plimmer, L. and Williams, A. (1999). *The 1999 Report on the Student Experience at UCE*. Birmingham: University of Central England.

Bowes, L., Harvey, L., Marlow-Hayes, N., Moon, S. and Plimmer, L. (2000). *The 2000 Report on the Student Experience at UCE*. Birmingham: University of Central England.

Geall, V., Moon, S., Harvey, L., Plimmer, L., Bowes, L. and Montague, G. (1996), *The 1996 Report on the Student Experience at UCE*. Birmingham: University of Central England.

Gibbs, P. (2006). 'Why assessment is changing'. In Bryan, C. and Clegg, K. (eds), *Innovative Assessment in Higher Education*. London: Routledge, pp. 11–22.

Green, D., Brannigan, C., Mazelan, P. and Giles, L. (1994). 'Measuring student satisfaction: a method of improving the quality of the student's experience'. In Haselgrove, S. (ed.), *The Student Experience*. Buckingham: Society for Research into Higher Education and Open University Press.

Harvey, J. (ed.) (1998). *Evaluation Cookbook*. Edinburgh: Heriot-Watt University. Available online at *http://www.icbl.hw.ac.uk/ltdi/cookbook/cookbook.pdf* (accessed 21 September 2009).

Harvey, L. (2003), 'Editorial: student feedback'. *Quality in Higher Education*, 9(1), 3–20.

Harvey, L., Moon, S. and Plimmer, L. (1997). *The Student Satisfaction Manual*. Buckingham: Society for Research into Higher Education and Open University Press.

Leckey, J. and Neill, N. (2001). 'Quantifying quality: the importance of student feedback'. *Quality in Higher Education*, 7(1), 19–32.

MacDonald, M., Saldaña, A. and Williams, J. (2003), *The 1996 Report on the Student Experience at UCE*. Birmingham: University of Central England.

MacDonald, M., Schwarz, J., Cappuccini, G., Kane, D., Gorman, P., Price, J., Sagu, S. and Williams, J., (2005). *The 2005 Report of the Student Experience at UCE*. Birmingham: University of Central England.

MacDonald, M., Williams, J., Gorman, P., Cappuccini-Ansfield, G., Kane, D. Schwarz, J. and Sagu, S. (2006). *The 2006 Report of the Student Experience at UCE*. Birmingham: University of Central England.

MacDonald, M., Williams, J., Kane, D., Gorman, P., Smith, E., Sagu, S. and Cappuccini-Ansfield, G. (2007). *The 2007 Report on the Student Experience at UCE Birmingham*. Birmingham: University of Central England.

MacDonald, M., Williams, J., Schwarz, J., Gorman, P., Mena, P. and Rawlins, L. (2004). *The 2004 Report of the Student Experience at UCE*. Birmingham: University of Central England.

Nilsson, K.-A. (2001). 'The action process of the student barometer: a profile of Lund University, Sweden'. In *Update: the Newsletter of the Centre for Research into Quality*, 15 (March).

Powney, J. and Hall, S. (1998). *Closing the Loop: The impact of student feedback on student feedback on students' subsequent learning*. Edinburgh: Scottish Council for Research in Education.

Richardson, J.T.E. (2005). 'Instruments for obtaining student feedback: a review of the literature'. *Assessment and Evaluation in Higher Education*, 30(4), 387–415.

Sheffield Hallam University (SHU) (2003). 'Student Experience Survey 2002 – feedback'. Sheffield: Sheffield Hallam University. Cited in Williams and Kane (2008).

University of Bath (2009). 'Learning and Teaching Enhancement Office: Student Satisfaction Survey 2003'. *University of Bath Website*. Available online at *http://www.bath.ac.uk/learningandteaching/surveys/ses/2003* (accessed 23 September 2009).

Watson, S. (2003). 'Closing the Feedback Loop: Ensuring effective action from student feedback'. *Tertiary Education and Management*, 9(2), 145–57.

Williams, J. and Kane, D. (2008). *Exploring the National Student Survey: assessment and feedback issues*. York: Higher Education Academy.

Williams, J. and Kane, D. (2009). 'Assessment and Feedback: Institutional Experiences of Student Feedback, 1996 to 2007', *Higher Education Quarterly* 63(3), 264–286.

Index